William Fairley

Epitaphiana

The Curiosities of Churchyard Literature

William Fairley
Epitaphiana
The Curiosities of Churchyard Literature
ISBN/EAN: 9783337004187

Printed in Europe, USA, Canada, Australia, Japan

Cover: Foto ©Thomas Meinert / pixelio.de

More available books at **www.hansebooks.com**

EPITAPHIANA:

OR,

The Curiosities of Churchyard Literature.

BEING A

MISCELLANEOUS COLLECTION OF EPITAPHS.

WITH AN

INTRODUCTION

GIVING AN ACCOUNT OF VARIOUS CUSTOMS PREVAILING AMONGST
THE ANCIENTS AND MODERNS IN THE DISPOSAL
OF THEIR DEAD.

BY

W. FAIRLEY, F.S.S.,

MINING ENGINEER, CERTIFICATED COLLIERY MANAGER, MEMBER OF THE MIDLAND
INSTITUTE OF MINING ENGINEERS, AUTHOR OF "THE COLLIERY MANAGER'S
CALCULATOR," "PRACTICAL OBSERVATIONS ON THE SOUTH WALES
COAL FIELD," "GLOSSARY OF TERMS USED IN THE COAL
MINING DISTRICTS OF SOUTH WALES, BRISTOL,
AND SOMERSETSHIRE," ETC., ETC.

London:
SAMUEL TINSLEY, PUBLISHER,
10, SOUTHAMPTON STREET, STRAND
1873.

All Rights of Translation and Reproduction reserved.]

Watson and Hazell, Printers, London and Aylesbury.

TO

MR. ALBAN CHIVERS,

OF WRITHLINGTON, SOMERSETSHIRE,

AS A MEMENTO OF MANY YEARS' FRIENDSHIP,

THIS LITTLE BOOK,

WITH SENTIMENTS OF RESPECT,

IS DEDICATED

BY

THE AUTHOR.

PREFACE.

AMIDST the multitudinous engagements of the writer he has, during the last twenty-two years, found time to collect the following curiosities of churchyards. The history of the collection might to some be interesting: it now forms a book of some bulk, but in its compilation only a minute or two now and then has been occupied. When the author has found himself in a village with a spare moment, he has frequently been engaged in perusing the literature of the churchyard. (Sometimes, much to his chagrin, he has been locked out, and so disallowed the indulgence of his desires.) Many curious verses have been thus collected in his travels up and down the country.

At first the curiosities collected were simply intended for the author's own private amusement; they have now, however, swollen to such proportions that he has been induced to give them to the world.

Here will be found the epitaphs of many noted persons, and some curious verses from all parts of the kingdom—the sad, serious, witty, and sublime have all found a place in the book; but, whilst the collection embraces many that are sufficiently ludicrous, care has been taken to keep out all that would be offensive to polite ears.

It has often been a matter of surprise to the writer that so much nonsense has been allowed to be engraved and erected in churchyards—showing, no doubt, that our clergymen have not that requisite authority in this matter which they should have. The burial-grounds of Roman Catholics are freer from such doggerel, from the fact that the priest supervises everything that is set up in their churchyards.

For the collection here brought before the public the writer does not claim that it is exhaustive, but that it forms an amusing miscellany, which may occasionally be read as an antidote to *ennui* by those who are suffering from that complaint.

W. FAIRLEY.

Lydney, 9*th*, *July*, 1873.

INTRODUCTION.

THE remarks which are made here are intended to convey a kind of general impression of how dead bodies have been disposed of at different times and places. In this, however, the writer wishes it to be distinctly understood that he does not profess to exhaust the subject—neither time, inclination, nor ability will allow him to undertake such a task; he has no doubt, however, that what is here stated will be found correct, and it may be accepted, as far as it goes, as a contribution to the subject.

COFFINS AND BANDAGES.

The custom of placing the dead in coffins

previous to burial was not prevalent, except with the Egyptians and Babylonians, in ancient times, as indeed it is not in some countries at the present time. When Lazarus was raised from the dead he was bound in *grave-clothes*, most likely such as are now used in Western Africa, where the practice is—not using coffins—to wrap the body in rolls of cloths, around the arms, legs, head, and feet: the ends of the cloth are sewed, or a narrow bandage is wound over the whole.

EMBALMING.

The practice of embalming dead bodies was very common amongst the Egyptians in ancient times. After Jacob's death his body was embalmed, and the Egyptians mourned for him seventy days. The *modus operandi* of embalming was to lay open the body, remove the intestines, and replace them with desiccative drugs and odoriferous spices.

The anointing of dead bodies previous to

interment was a custom prevailing amongst the Jews, and no doubt our Saviour referred to it when he said to the woman who poured a very precious ointment on his His head (Matt. xxvi. 12), "*She did it for my burial.*"

CEMETERIES.

Like our cemeteries of the present day, the Jewish burial-grounds were at a small distance from their cities and villages. The graves of the principal citizens were distinguished by having cupolas, or vaulted chambers, of three, four, or more square yards, built over them; these frequently lay open, and afforded to passers-by shelter from the inclemency of the weather—hence the expression (Mark v. 3), "dwelling among the tombs."

The places which the Hebrews appropriated for the burial of their dead were both public and private. Thus, in the twenty-third chapter of Genesis, we read that Abraham had for a possession the field of Machpelah as a burying-place; and again we read (Judges viii. 32) that Joash had a sepulchre, in which Gideon his son was buried; and Samson was interred in the burying-place of his father Manoah (Judges xvi. 31). Asahel, likewise, was buried in the sepulchre of his father, which was in Bethlehem (2 Sam. ii. 32). The bones of Saul and Jonathan his son were buried in the country of Benjamin, in Zelah, in the sepulchre of Kish, his father (2 Sam. xxi. 14). So much for the private burial-places. Reference is made to public cemeteries in 2 Kings xxiii. 6, where we read of "the graves of the children of the people"; and in Jeremiah xxvi. 23 we learn that the dead body of Urijah was *cast* into the graves of the common people.

CAVES.

The places of sepulture of the Jews were selected sometimes in gardens or fields, but more generally in hollow places, or in rocks or caves, and their sepulchres were whitewashed, for the sake of ornament and to prevent illness.

The tombs in the necropolis of Sela were cut out of the sides of the rock surrounding the ancient city.

The tombs of the prophets, referred to by our Saviour in Matt. xxiv. 29, situated on the western declivity of the Mount of Olives, are large excavations having numerous cells to deposit bodies in.

The sides of the Valley of Jehoshaphat are everywhere studded with tombs excavated in the rocks.

The tombs of the kings, near Jerusalem, exhibit the remains of a magnificent edifice excavated from the solid rock (Bastow).

TUMULI.

The tumuli, mounds, or barrows, which have been found, we might almost say, in all quarters of the globe, are said to be the most ancient and general of all monuments to the dead: the researches of archæologists of the present day show that they were places in which the ancients deposited their dead. The earliest we read of is that which was erected over the remains of Patroclus, the friend of Achilles, and in whose memory the Greeks established solemn funeral games. In the mounds of various parts of Assyria and Mesopotamia funeral vases and glazed earthen coffins are found piled up in great numbers.

PYRAMIDS.

It is conjectured by some that the Egyptian Pyramids were erected for sepulchral purposes: the largest one is that which is supposed to contain the bones of Cheops, and we have read somewhere that 100,000 men worked without interruption for twenty years in building this enormous pyramid.

MAUSOLEUMS.

The word mausoleum, now used to signify a sepulchral edifice, is from Mausolus, the King of Caria, who died 353 years before Christ, and whose Queen, Artemisia, caused to be erected to his memory the most splendid sepulchral monument the world had seen, which was esteemed one of the seven wonders of the world.

BURNING THE DEAD.

It has been customary in many countries to burn the dead, and to collect the ashes in urns. This custom of reducing the remains to ashes by fire still prevails in some parts, as will be seen in the sequel.

PERSIAN CUSTOMS.

The Guebers, or fire-worshippers, in Persia, do not bury their dead, but expose the bodies on rocks or the towers of their temples, to be eaten by birds.

CUSTOMS AT SOUTH AFRICA.

The burial customs of South Africa are singular: thus, in the country around Pungo Andongo the ancient burial-places of the Jinga are said to be simply large mounds of stones, with drinking and cooking utensils of rude pottery on them.

The monuments are sometimes built up in a circular form, like hay-cocks, and contain no inscriptions. Amongst the people cross-roads seem to be much liked as sites for burial purposes.*

CUSTOMS AT NAPLES.

In Naples the disposition of the dead appears to be according to the wealth or poverty of the living, and the remains of one who dies without possessions are treated in a "raw" and "uncultivated" manner. There are here two cemeteries, viz., Campo Santo Nuovo and Campo

---

* For detailed particulars see Dr. Livingstone's Travels in Africa, pp. 359, 424, etc.

Santo Vecchio, both on the north-east side of the city, situated not far from each other.

Campo Santo Nuovo is situated on an eminence commanding a beautiful view of the city and the mountains: we might compare it to a garden full of shady trees and flowers, which fill the air with sweet narcotic perfumes. Here the grave monuments are to be seen in the form of streets, and arrange themselves in rows on both sides. Others stand isolated in groups, or like a small death-town. In Campo Santo Nuovo there are three classes of funerals, which are carried out with more or less luxury, according to the price: the third class, for the poor, consists in simply placing the dead into a coffin—which is carried into effect at a cost of twenty francs. Those, however, who do not leave behind them this sum cannot be buried in Campo Santo Nuovo, but must be interred in Campo Santo Vecchio: this is the great paupers' churchyard of Naples; whoever may have witnessed a funeral here will not be likely to call the churchyard holy ground, but will compare it with a field where scavengers' sweepings are deposited, as the remains are here carelessly tipped out; and this kind of funeral ceremony is performed by the Neapolitan Corporation.*

CUSTOMS OF THE NORTH-WESTERN AMERICAN INDIANS.

In lieu of coffins boxes are used, into which the bodies are doubled, which, however, are not placed underground, but up trees: around the boxes are hung the property of the deceased, blankets, etc. Another way is to put the box into a tent, or house, with trinkets and household implements around, the box being supported by trestles. A third method is to place the body in a canoe. "On an island in the Columbia River there used to be quite a collection of canoes with such freights; and Deadman's Island, in Victoria

---

* See article " Eine Statte des Entsetzens," in Garten Laube.

Harbour, is another place where many of the bodies are placed in canoes."

It is likewise customary amongst the Tsunpsheans, the Takali, and most of the Southern Oregonia and Californian tribes, to burn the body, and either bury or hang up the ashes in the lodge: with the body is burnt the deceased's broken canoes, and such of his blankets as are not sold.*

THE CATACOMBS OF ROME.

These subterraneous galleries are both singular and interesting, and offer the most valuable sources of study both to the archæologist and theologian: here we learn the condition of the Christians in primitive times. These underground galleries were used as Christian places of burial, refuge, and worship from the end of the first century. There are about sixty catacombs, the largest

---

* For a fuller description of these customs see Dr. Robert Brown's new and excellent work, the "Races of Mankind," pp. 107 to 111.

of which has twenty miles of galleries, which branched off in every direction under the Campania.

Altogether there are about 500 miles of passages, containing about six millions of graves. Some of the underground chambers were decorated with coloured paintings, which gave interesting pictures of the system of the catacombs—which were not used exclusively by Christians, but by Jews and Pagans as well.

By a survey of these subterraneous passages we learn two great facts, *viz.*, that the ancient Christians left no evidence that they worshipped martyrs or the Virgin Mary, or that they entertained the supremacy of the Pope. It was customary for both Pagans and Christians to put the emblems of their trade upon their tombs.

INSCRIPTIONS.

That inscriptions on sepulchres were used in early times may be inferred from the 16th and

17th verses of the xxiii. chap. of 2 Kings. Amongst the Greeks the honour of an inscription was only paid to the tomb of a hero.

The tombs of the Romans were usually situated on the highway, and those who consecrated a tomb to their relations had the privilege of writing thereon. Many of their epitaphs commenced with "Sta, viator!" to attract the attention of passers-by, which expression is to this day imitated by the English, who commence many of their verses with the words, *Stop reader!*

The epitaphs of the Romans were brief, simple, and familiar—three qualities which have been considered very desirable in this kind of literature, and which might be introduced into other classes with benefit.

The custom of placing inscriptions on tombs was introduced into England by the Romans, after their invasion of this country. Up to the end of the twelfth century Latin prevails on the tombs; during the thirteenth and fourteenth centuries French was used; but after that time the vernacular came into general use.

The inscriptions on the tombs of the present day are of a very varied character, as we shall show in the following pages.

GERMAN CUSTOMS.

The custom of inserting in the newspapers a special advertisement recording the death of friends is very common throughout Germany. The writer has just met with one of these announcements, which, even for that country, is singular. The *Leipzeger Tageblatt*, in a recent number, records a death in the following manner:—

"The day before yesterday, at the sixth hour, died my dearly beloved wife Pauline, maiden name Vorgt, after a short illness and six months of married happiness, in the 24th year of her age. Whoever knew her will be able to estimate my grief. Moritz Knofel prays for sympathy.

N.B.—The business of my dear wife, at the weekly

market, will be carried on as usual."—From *Londoner Zeitung*, 14th June, 1873.

Like that of England, the churchyard literature is very various, and occasionally very droll. (See No. 346.)

EPITAPHIAN LITERATURE.

There are several books already before the public, written exclusively on epitaphian subjects. We may mention a few for example:—Webb's "Epitaphs," Pulleyn's Collection, "Wandler unter Gräbern, von Prediger, Hatzler," Freiburg, 1817. Weber speaks of a " Launigten Gräbschriften " of 1786, of which we cannot state any particulars; and there is an old book called "Epitaphia jocoseria latina, gallica, italica, hispanica, lusitanica et belgica, collegit T. Swertius, Antwerp, 1645 ": two-thirds of this collection is in Latin, and many of the examples given are considered good. In Carl Julius Weber's "Demokritos" there is an essay entitled, "Weber Komische Gräbschriften," from which a little matter has been borrowed in the writing of this introduction. The writer remembers having seen other collections, but cannot bring to mind, whilst he is writing, the correct titles of them.

In the "Poet's Orchard," a poetical work by the Rev. Thos. Marsden, there are several original epitaphs given, which are remarkable for nothing perhaps excepting their simplicity. The following is a fair specimen :—

> Within this grave
> Lies William Brave.

For more of the same sort the reader is referred to the work itself.

Verses and quotations are often misplaced on tombstones. Charles Lamb, in a letter to Wordsworth, 19th October, 1810, gives an example of this sort, where he says that in Islington churchyard is to be seen an epitaph on an infant who died "Ætatis four months," with the following inscription appended: "Honour thy father and thy mother, that thy days may be long in the land," etc.! The following is another specimen of the same description, copied by the writer from a stone in Pembrey churchyard: at first sight it was supposed to be a verse of poetry; it turned out, however, to be four lines of Scripture and John Bunyan jumbled together:—

> Set thine house in order,
> For thou shalt die.
> Christian at the sight of
> Cross loses his burden.

Lamb was not pleased with the nonsense that was to be met with in his day on tombstones, and in his New Year's Eve said, "I conceive disgust at those impertinent and misbecoming familiarities inscribed upon your ordinary tombstones." He evidently thought burial subjects should be treated in a more serious manner: he once said in a letter to Bernard Barton, 17th September, 1823, that "satire does not look pretty upon a tombstone." He wanted the inscriptions to contain some useful lessons to the living, and in a letter to Mr. Coleridge, dated October 23rd, 1802, says, "When men go off the stage so early, it scarce seems a noticeable thing in their epitaphs whether they had been wise or silly in their lifetime." We love to dwell on all that he has said on this subject, for there is always a heartiness about his expressions. Of his fine feelings and chaste words the following is an example. In a letter to Mr. Manning he sent an epitaph which he scribbled over on a "poor girl, who died at nineteen, a good girl, and a pretty girl, and a clever girl, but strangely neglected by all her friends:"—

> Under this cold marble stone
> Sleep the sad remains of one
> Who, when alive, by few or none
> Was loved, as loved she might have been,
> If she prosperous days had seen,
> Or had thriving been, I ween.

Only this cold funeral stone
Tells she was beloved by one
Who on the marble graves his moan.

Women sometimes wish for an opportunity to be revenged on their husbands. As an example of this we may relate that the wife of a man named Baldwin, of Lymington, Hampshire, had made a vow " to dance over his grave "—they had not lived happily together. To defeat her design Baldwin left special instructions that his body should be sunk in the sea in Scratchall's Bay, off the Needles, Isle of Wight; and it appears his body was so disposed of on the 20th May, 1736, as the parochial register of Lymington records.

Many epitaphs are repeated in different churchyards; and as to "Affliction sore long time I bore," the writer does not know where it is not to be found, as many as a dozen copies of it having been found in some churchyards. The blacksmith's epitaph : " My sledge and hammer lie declined," may be found in Carisbrooke, Isle of Wight, Felpham in Sussex, Westham in Essex, Chipping Sodbury, and Houghton, Hunts.

"She was but reason forbids me to say what," although a strange verse for a gravestone, is to be found in several places—as Monkwearmouth, Swansea, Clerkenwell, Lambeth, and Bolton. (See Nos. 4, 189, 292, 329, and 337.)

The provincialism of a district may frequently be detected in country churchyards; thus, when the poet rhymes *praise* with *rise*, we may be pretty sure in guessing him to be a Gloucestershire man, though we might be unable to fix him at Wapley, where the lines are engraved. The verse runs thus :—

> Now at that great and joyful day,
>   When all men must arise,
> I hope to be amongst the just,
>   A singing of His praise.

The same thing may be detected at Berkeley,

where the poet makes *day* and *key* to rhyme. (See 356.)

Of epigrammatic epitaphs there are many: that on a Cardinal is the best we have met with :—

> Here lies a Cardinal, who wrought
>   Both good and evil in his time ;
> The good he did was good for nought ;
>   Not so the *evil!* that was prime.

In Bath Abbey is to be found the following gentle piece of satire :—

> These walls, adorned with monumental bust,
> Shew how Bath waters serve to lay the dust.

A couplet which reminds us of the Cheltenham epitaph :—

> Here lies I and my three daughters,
> Kill'd by drinking Cheltenham waters ;
> Had we a' stuck to Epsom-salts
> We'd not a bin lying in these 'ere vaults.

And not to burden our readers with French

epitaphs, we are tempted to give one, which is, like many others, very amusing :—

> Ci-gît mon oncle Etienne,
> S'il est bien, qu'il s'y tienne ! *

There is in Erfurt an interesting epitaph, of which Luther speaks in his " Table Talk," and which is grounded on a historical fact :—

> Hier unter diesem. Stein
> Liegt begraben allein
> Der Vater und seine Tochter,
> Der Bruder und seine Schwester,
> Der Mann und sein Weib.
> Und sein doch nur zwei Leib ! †

---

* Which may be freely rendered thus :—

> Beneath our feet lies dear old uncle Stephen,
> If he's all right, he will not be for leaving !

† Here, beneath this stone,
  Lie buried alone
  The father and his daughter.
  The brother and his sister,
  The man and his wife,
  And only two bodies.

Without attempting an explanation, we leave this riddle to be solved by our readers, after which they may peruse the French one, No. 124 of this collection.

There is satire in that on a German Doctor:—

> Hier, ruht mein lieber Arzt, Herr Grimm,
> Und, die er heilte, neben ihm.*

And the couplet following is not without some wit :—

> Befreie doch mich arme Gruft,
> O Wanderer, von diesem Schuft! †

Both the English and the French have a parellel for the German lines which record the calm state of mind of a bereaved husband :—

---

* Here lies my adviser, Dr. Grimm,
And those he healed—near him.

† In this case a literal translation cannot be given in rhyme, but it may be rendered thus :—

> We hope the wanderer now is willing
> To free the grave from this great villain.

Mein Weib deck't dieser Grabstein zu,
Für ihre und für meine Ruh!*

---

    * Here lies my wife,
        A fact that must tell
    For her repose
        And for mine as well.

EPITAPHIANA.

1. From Preston Churchyard, near Weymouth:—

> One and forty years
>   In wedlock we have been;
> Ten children we have had,
>   But one is to be seen.

2. On an Avaricious Man:—

> At rest beneath this churchyard stone
>   Lies stingy JEMMY WYATT;
> He died one morning just at ten, and
>   Saved a dinner by it.

3. From Bideford Churchyard:—

> The wedding-day appointed was
>   And wedding clothes provided;
> But ere that day did come, alas!
>   He sickened, and he—dided!

4. From Monkwearmouth Churchyard :—

In Memory oF Sarah WiLLock WiFe of John Willock. Wo Died August 15, 1825, Aged 48 Years, She was But Reason ForBids me to Sa what But think what a woman should Be and she was that. (See 189, 292.)

5. From a Graveyard in Cheraw, South Carolina, and elsewhere :—

> My name, my country, what are they to thee?
> What, whether high or low my pedigree?
> Perhaps I far surpassed all other men;
> Perhaps I fell below them all,—what then?
> Suffice it, stranger, that thou seest a tomb;
> Thou know'st its use : it hides—no matter whom.

6. From a Welsh Churchyard :—

> Life is an inn upon a market-day :
> Some short-pursed pilgrims breakfast and away;
> Some do to dinner stay, and get full fed,
> And others after supper steal to bed;
> Large are the bills who linger out the day,
> The shortest stayers have the least to pay.

7. From Llangerrig Churchyard, Montgomeryshire :—

> O earth, O earth, observe this well—
> That earth to earth shall come to dwell;
> Then earth in earth shall close remain
> Till earth from earth shall rise again.

8. From the same place :—

> From earth my body first arose
> But here to earth again it goes,
> I never desire to have it more
> To plague me as it did before.

9. The following lines, said to have been written by SHAKESPEARE, are inscribed on a flat stone which marks the spot where he is buried in the churchyard of Stratford-on-Avon :—

> Good friend, for Jesus' sake forbeare
> To dig the dust enclosèd here.
> Blessed be he that spares these stones,
> And curst be he that moves my bones.

10. On a Country Sexton :—

> Here lies old HARE, worn out with care,
>   Who whilom tolled the bell;
> Could dig a grave, or set a stave,
>   And say Amen full well.

> For sacred songs he'd Sternhold's tongue,
>   And Hopkin's eke also;
> With cough and hem he stood by them,
>   As far as lungs would go.
> Many a feast for worms he drest,
>   Himself then wanting bread;
> But, lo! he's gone, with skin and bone
>   To starve 'em now he's dead.
> Here take his spade, and use his trade,
>   Since he is out of breath;
> Cover the bones of him who once
>   Wrought journey-work for Death.

11. On a Baker:—

> RICHARD FULLER lies buried here;
> Do not withhold the crystal tear;
> For when he lived he daily fed
> Woman, and man, and child with bread,
> But now, alas! he's turn'd to dust,
> As thou, and I, and all soon must;
> And lies beneath this turf so green,
> Where worms do daily feed on him.

12. On JOHN SO.

The following lines were some years ago found among the papers of an old man of the name of John So, who passed the greater part of his life in obscurity, within a few miles of Port Glasgow; and the handwriting leads to the conclusion that it was written by himself:—

>So died JOHN SO,
>So so did he so?
>So did he live,
>And so did he die;
>So so did he so?
>And so let him lie.

13. *On the Provost of Dundee.*

Some years since a MR. DICKSON, who was provost of Dundee, in Scotland, died, and by will left the sum of one guinea to a person to compose an epitaph upon him; which sum he directed his three executors to pay. The executors, thinking to defraud the poet, agreed to meet and share the guinea amongst them, each contributing a line to the epitaph, which ran as follows:—

>*First.*—Here lies DICKSON, Provost of Dundee.
>*Second.*—Here lies Dickson, Here lies he.

The third was put to it for a long time, but unwilling to lose his share of the guinea, vociferously bawled out:—

  · Hallelujah—halleluje.

14. From Marnhull Churchyard:—

  Remember me as you pass by;
  As you are now so once was I.
  As I am now, so you must be,
  Therefore prepare to follow me.

Underneath these lines some one wrote in blue paint:—

  To follow you I'm not content,
  Unless I knew which way you went.

15. On an Innkeeper at Eton:—

  Life's an inn, my house will show it—
  I thought so once, but now I know it.
  Man's life is but a winter's day:
  Some only breakfast and away;
  Others to dinner stay, and are full fed;
  The oldest man but sups and then to bed;
  Large is his debt who lingers out the day;
  He who goes soonest has the least to pay.

There is more than one example of this epitaph extant. No. 6 appears to be an abbreviation of it. The two first lines here are like the epitaph said to have been written by Gay. (See No. 171.)

16. On a Lawyer and his Client :—

> God works wonders now and then :
> Here lies a lawyer and an honest man.

Answered :—

> This is a mere law quibble, not a wonder :
> Here lies a lawyer, and his client under.

17. From a Churchyard in Devonshire :—

> For me deceased, weep not, my dear ;
> I am not dead, but sleepeth here ;
> Your time will come—prepare to die ;
> Wait but a while, you'll follow I.

18. From a Burial-ground in the Crimea ;

Sacred to the memory of FREDERICK SPRATT, private, Royal Marines, late of Her Majesty's Ship *Bellerophon*, who departed this life on the 21st April, 1855, at the age of 36 years :—

Here lies an old soldier, whom all must applaud:
He fought many battles both at home and abroad;
But the fiercest engagement he ever was in,
Was the battle of self in the conquest of sin.

19. By GEORGE JOBLIN, Shoemaker, of Wallsend, intended for his own tombstone:—

My cutting-boards to pieces split,
My size-stick measures no more feet,
My lasts are broke all into holes,
My blunted knife cuts no more holes,
My fuddling caps to thrums are wore,
My apron is to tie my store,
My welt ties out, my awls are broken,
And merry glees are all forgotten.
No more I'll use black ball or rozin,
My copperas and my shop-tub's frozen.
No more I'll have occasion for course of work,
Nor count dead horse, or kick the kirk.
My pinchers are with age grown smooth,
And   bones grow little worth;
My lapstone's broke, my colour's done,
My gum-glass's broke, my paste is run,
My hammer-head's broke off the shaft;
No more Saint-Monday with the craft.
My nippers, tack, strap, and rag,

And all my kit has got the bag;
My ends are sewn, my pegs are driven,
And now I'm on the tramp to heaven.

20. From Houghton Churchyard, Hunts:—

My sledge and hammer lie declined,
My bellows, too, have lost their wind;
My fire is spent, my forge decay'd,
My vice is on the dust all laid;
My coal is spent, my iron gone,
My nails are drove, my work is done;
My fire-dried corpse here lies at rest,
My soul, smoke-like, soars to be blest.

21. On an Italian:—

I was well,
Wished to be better,
Took physic and died!

22. Counsel to all:—

Live well—die never:
Die well—live for ever.

This is said to be in Kingston Churchyard, Hants.

23. On E. N. :—

At the Ester end of this free stone here doeth ly the Letle Bone of Walter Spurrer that fine boy that was his friends only joy. He was Drouned at Melhams Bridg. the 20th of August 1691.

24. On an Infidel :—

> Here lies a dicer long in doubt
> If death could kill his soul or not;
> Here ends his doubtfulness, at last
> Convinced—but, oh! the die is cast!

25. From a Grindstone now in use near Bridgehouse :—

Here lies the body of FANNY, the daughter of John Howard, who departed this life the 8th day of February, 1774, in the fifth year of her age.

The explanation given is that the gravestone was carried by a flood in the Calder from Pipponden to the spot near which it is now used.

26. From a pane of glass of a Somersetshire Inn :—

Here lies TOMMY MONTAGUE,
Whose love for angling daily grew ;
He died regretted, while late out,
To make a capture of a trout.

27. From Ockham Churchyard :—

Though many a sturdy oak he laid along,
Felled by Death's surer hatchet, here lies SPONG.
Posts he oft made, yet ne'er a place could get,
And lived by *railing*, though he had no wit.
Old saws he had, although no antiquarian ;
And *stiles* corrected, yet was no grammarian.

28. On a Watchmaker, in Lydford Churchyard, on the borders of Dartmoor :—

Here lies, in horizontal position,
the outside case of
GEORGE ROUTLEIGH, watchmaker ;
Whose abilities in that line were an honour
to his profession.
Integrity was the Mainspring, and prudence the
Regulator,
of all the actions of his life.
Humane, generous, and liberal,
his Hand never stopped

till he had relieved distress.
So nicely regulated were all his motions,
that he never went wrong,
except when set a-going
by people
who did not know his Key:
even then he was easily
set right again.
He had the art of disposing his time so well
that his hours glided away
in one continual round
of pleasure and delight,
till an unlucky minute put a period to
his existence.
He departed this life
Nov. 14, 1802,
aged 57:
wound up,
in hopes of being taken in hand
by his Maker;
and of being thoroughly cleaned, repaired,
and set a-going
in the world to come.

29. On a Miser:—

Here lies one who lived unloved, and died unlamented

who denied plenty to himself, assistance to his friends, and relief to the poor; who starved his family, oppressed his neighbours, and plagued himself to gain what he could not enjoy. At last, Death, more merciful to him than he was to himself, released him from care, and his family from want; and here he lies with the unknown he imitated, and with the soil he loved, in fear of a resurrection, lest his heirs should have spent the money he left behind, having laid up no treasure where moth and rust do not corrupt, or thieves break through and steal.

30. From Royton Churchyard.

JOHN KAY, a Lancashire mathematician, died on the 31st December, 1824, in the 43rd year of his age. His remains were interred in Royton Churchyard, and the place where he rests is marked by a plain stone, bearing the following inscription:—

> In mathematics soared his noble mind,
> Peace robed his soul—he felt for all mankind;
> He loved true virtue, but disliked vain pride;
> Truth was his aim, and reason was his guide.

31. On a Miser (See Nos. 2, 29, etc.):—

> Iron was his chest,
> Iron was his door,
> His head was iron,
> And his heart was more.

32. On a London Cook:—

> Peas to his Hashes;
> meaning of course,
> Peace to his ashes.

33. From Bath.

On the interior walls of the Widcombe Church, Bath, are a few monuments of interest, from which the following, dated February, 1610, is taken:—

> Die Februari, 1610.
> JANE GAY, of Eyles, here lies under this,
> Whom many loved living, whom died many mise;
> A wife she was, of right honest skill,—
> Though here she lyes dead, her fame liveth still.

In the present Church of St. Mary Magdalen, of the same city, which was repaired in 1760, and again enlarged by the addition of a chancel in the years 1823 and 1824, is a small building erected by Prior Cantlow, between the years 1489 and 1499, with a small battlemented turret for a bell at the west end, and a south porch, in which is the following incised inscription in black letter :—

Thys. chapell. floryschyd wt. formasyte. spectabyll.
  In. the. honore. of M. Magdalene. prior Cantlow. hath edyfyed.
Desyring. you. to. pray. for. hym wt. youre. pr'yers. delectabyll.
  That. sche. will. inhabyt. hym. in. hevyn. there. ever. to abyde.

34. From a Tombstone in Ireland :—

>Here lies the body of JOHN MOUND,
>Lost at sea and never found.

This is comparable with the Welsh one, No. 176.

35. From a Cemetery near Cincinnati :—

>Here lies ———,
>who came to this city and died
>*for the benefit of his health.*

36. From an Irish Churchyard.

Patrick O'Brien was one day strolling with a friend through a graveyard, when his eye was arrested by an epitaph which shocked his sense of propriety and veracity: it ran thus:—

> Weep not for me, my children dear;
> I am not dead, but sleeping here.

"Well," said Paddy, "if I was dead I should be honest enough to own it."

37. From America.

Both the Irish and Americans give us something to laugh at when they handle epitaphian matters. The following is from a tombstone in Oxford, New Hampshire:—

> To all my friends I bid adieu;
> A more sudden death you never knew;
> As I was leading the old mare to drink,
> She kick'd and kill'd me quicker 'n a wink.

In Whitby Churchyard there is an epitaph, the

sentiment of which is very similar to this. (See No. 194.)

38. From St. Peter's Churchyard, Barton:—

> Doom'd to receive half my soul held dear,
> The other half with grief she left me here.
> Ask not her name for she was true and just;
> Once a fine woman, now a heap of dust.

No name is recorded on the stone, but the year 1777 is given as the date. A curious and romantic legend attaches to the epitaph. In the above year an unknown lady of great beauty, who was conjectured to have loved "not wisely, but too well," came to reside in the town. She was accompanied by a gentleman, who left her after making lavish arrangements for her comfort. She was proudly reserved in her manners, frequently took long solitary walks, and studiously avoided all intercourse. She died in giving birth to a child, and without disclosing her name or family connexions. After her decease, the gentleman who came with her arrived, and was overwhelmed with grief at the intelligence which awaited him. He took the child away without unravelling the secret, having first ordered the stone to be erected, and delivered into the mason's hands the verse, which is at once a mystery and a memento.

39. On Lord Brougham.

It is said that this distinguished nobleman, once in a playful mood, wrote the following epitaph for himself:—

> Here, reader, turn your weeping eyes,
>   My fate a useful moral teaches;
> The hole in which my body lies
>   Would not contain one half my speeches.

40. From a Montgomeryshire Churchyard.

In this churchyard there are some remarkably large yew trees; beneath one of them is a gravestone with the following inscription :—

> Under this yew-tree
> Buried would I be,
> For my father and me
> Planted this yew-tree.

41. From Gloucester.

On a youth of the name of CALF, who was buried in Gloucester Cathedral:—

> Oh, cruel death, more subtle than the Fox,
> To kill this CALF before he came an Ox!
>
> (Note by W. F.)

The writer has an idea that there is a German epitaph similar to this, as there certainly is one in French:—

> Ci-gît le jeune JEAN LE VEAU
> Sans devenir Bœuf ou Taureau.

Which may be rendered:—

> JOHN CALF, junior, lieth here,
> Without becoming Ox or Steer.

42. On a Poet:—

> Here let a bard unenvied rest,
> Who no dull critic dares molest;

Escaped from the familiar ills
Of thread-bare coat and unpaid bills;
From rough bum-bailiffs' upstart duns,
From sneering pride's detested sons,
From all those pest'ring ills of life,
From, worse than all, a *scolding wife*.

43. On a Surgeon :—

Here lies in repose, after great deeds of blood,
　An hospital surgeon thorough,
Who bled for his own and his country's good,
　And St. Thomas's Hospital, Borough.

44. From Hordle, near Lymington.

The Poacher's Friend.—In the churchyard of Hordle there was erected, in 1858, a granite obelisk to the memory of the late J. COLLETT, Esq., who will be remembered for his strong antagonism to the Game Laws, supporting his views by almost indiscriminately paying the fines inflicted on parties convicted of poaching whose cases were brought under his notice. Besides recording the date of his death, etc., the obelisk has the following inscription :—

>Ci-gît l'ami du Braconnier.
>Here lies the friend of the poacher.

45. From Bath Abbey :—

>Near this place
>lie interred the remains of MARY
>ANN, second Daughter
>of George Watts, Esq., and Ann his wife,
>who died (after a lingering illness)
>February 14th, 1813, Aged 15.
>She lived beloved
>And died lamented.

46. On LADY MILLER, in Bath Abbey :—

>Near this monument are deposited the Remains of
>LADY MILLER,
>Wife to Sir John Miller, Bart., of Bath-Easton Villa.
>She departed this life, at the Hotwells of Bristol, the 24th
>June, 1781, in the Forty-first year of her Age.

>Devoted Stone! amidst the wrecks of Time,
>Uninjured bear thy *Miller's* spotless Name :

The Virtues of her Youth, and ripen'd Prime,
  The tender thought, th' enduring Record claim.

When clos'd the numerous eyes that round this Bier
  Have wept the Loss of wide-extended Worth;
O, gentle Stranger, may one gen'rous Tear
  Drop, as thou bendest o'er this hallow'd Earth.

Are Truth and Genius, Love and Pity, thine?
  With lib'ral Charity, and Faith sincere?
Then rest thy wandering Step beneath this shrine;
  And greet a kindred Spirit hov'ring near.

47. On JAMES QUIN, in Bath Abbey.

Underneath his bust is the following inscription :—

OB: MDCCLXVI.

ÆTAT: LXXIII.

That tongue *which set the table on a roar*,
And charm'd the public ear, is heard no more:
Clos'd are those eyes, the harbinger of wit,
Which spake before the tongue what SHAKESPEAR
  writ:
Cold is that hand, which living was stretched forth,
At friendship's call, to succour modest worth;

Here lies JAMES QUIN: deign, reader, to be taught,
Whate'er thy strength of body, force of thought,
In nature's happiest mould however cast,
To this complexion thou must come at last.

D. GARRICK.

48. On JOHN COLLIER, *alias* TIM BOBBIN, the Lancashire Poet.

He was a native of Rochdale, and his tombstone bears the following inscription:—

> Here lies JOHN, and likewise MARY,
> Cheek by jowl and never weary;
> No wonder they so well agree,
> John wants no punch, nor Moll no tea.

49. On MARGERY SCOTT, in the Churchyard of Dalkeith, near Edinburgh:—

> Stop! Reader, stop! until my life you've read;
> The living may gain knowledge from the dead.
> Five times five years I lived a virgin's life,
> Ten times five years I was a virtuous wife,
> Ten times five years I lived a widow chaste,
> Now tired of this mortal life—I rest.

I from my cradle to my grave have seen
Eight mighty Kings of Scotland, and a Queen;
Four times five years the Commonwealth I saw,
Ten times the subjects rose against the Law.
Twice did I see the old Palaces pulled down,
And twice the cloak was humbled by the gown;
An end of Stewart's vivid law—nay, more,
I saw my country sold for English ore.
Such desolations in my time have been,
I have an end of all perfection seen.

50. On FRANCIS GROSE.

Grose was an Author of some Topographical works—a fact which gave the writer of his epitaph the opportunity of punning as follows:—

> Here lies FRANCIS GROSE.
> On Thursday, May 12, 1791,
> Death put an end to
> His *views* and *prospects!*

51. From old Grey Friars, at Edinburgh:—

> Here snug in grave my wife doth lie;
> Now she's at rest and so am I.

Several epitaphs of a similar description are to be met with in different parts of the world—52, for example, is from our Antipodes. No. 53 may, however, have the preference, as it is simply a quotation from the Sacred Scriptures.

52. From an Australian Graveyard :—

> Here lies my wife POLLY, a terrible shrew;
> If I said I was sorry, I should lie too.

According to Major Austin, this is to be seen in Père-la-Chaise.

53. From a Churchyard in Sussex :—

> Here lies the body of SARAH, wife of John ——,
> who died 24th March, 1823, aged 42 years.
> "The Lord giveth, and the Lord TAKETH AWAY:
> blessed be the name of the Lord."

54. I have not been able to trace the origin of the following, so give it merely as it was communicated to me :—

> Here lies my wife EDIE,
> Who in her time made me giddy;

>Here she lies without bed or blanket,
>As dead as a door-nail,—the Lord be thankéd.

55. On Honest Ned :—

>Here lies Honest Ned,
>Because he is dead.
>Had it been his father,
>We had much rather;
>Had it been his mother,
>We had rather than the other;
>Had it been his sister,
>We ne'er should have miss'd her:
>But since it is only Ned,
>There's no more to be said.

It is said that a similar epitaph was suggested for Frederick, Prince of Wales, the father of George III. (See likewise No. 103.)

56. From the Cathedral Yard, Winchester :—

>Here rests in peace a Hampshire grenadier,
>Who killed himself by drinking poor small beer.
>Soldiers, be warned by his untimely fall,
>And when you're hot drink strong, or none at all.

The memorial having fallen into decay in 1781,

it was then restored at the expense of some officers, who added the following couplet:—

> An honest soldier never is forgot,
> Whether he die by musquet or by pot.

57. From a Welsh Churchyard:—

> Two lovely babes lie buried here,
> As ever bless'd their parents dear;
> But they were seized with ague fits,
> And here they lie as dead as nits.

58. On DANIEL SAUL, formerly in St. Dunstan's, Stepney:—

> Here lies the body of DANIEL SAUL,
> Spitalfields weaver—and that's all.

A similar couplet is to be found in Addison's *Spectator*:—

> Here lies JOHN HALL,
> Spitalfields weaver—and that's all.

59. From a Graveyard near Birmingham:—

Oh, cruel Death! why wert thou so unkind,
To take the one, and leave the other behind?
Thou should'st have taken both or neither,
Which would have been more agreeable to the survivor.

60. From Grantham Churchyard:—

> JOHN PALFRYMAN, which lieth here,
> Was agéd twenty-four year;
> And near this place his mother lies,
> Also his father when he dies.

61. From a Churchyard near Salisbury:—

> Oh! Sun, Moon, Stars, and ye celestial Poles!
> Are graves, then, dwindled into *Button-holes?*

62. On DR. BANCROFT, Archbishop of Canterbury.

He was of a very covetous disposition,—a fact that appears not to have been overlooked in writing his epitaph:—

> Here lies his Grace, in cold clay clad,
> Who died for want of what he had.

63. From Chichester Cathedral. On a Crier of Periwinkles:—

"Periwinks, Periwinkles!" was ever her cry;
She laboured to live, poor and honest to die.
At the last day again how her old eyes will twinkle!
For no more will she cry, "Periwinks, Periwinkle!"
Ye rich, to virtuous want regard pray give;
Ye poor, by her example, learn to live.
          Died Jan. 1, 1786, Aged 77.

64. On Miss Long :—

She was a beautiful young lady, but so short that she was, when alive, called the "Pocket Venus." The epitaph concluded, alluding to her when alive :—

Though LONG, yet short,
Though short, yet *pretty* Long.

65. From St. Paul's, Covent Garden. On Mr. James Worsdale :—

Eager to get, but not to keep the pelf,
A friend to all mankind—except himself.

As a contrast to this we submit the following:—

66. On a Miser :—

Here lies old SPARGES,
Who died to save charges.

67. On ROBERT BURNS.

Robert Burns was born on the 25th of January, 1759, on the banks of the Doon, about two miles from Ayr. He died at Dumfries on the 21st of July, 1796, aged 37 years and about 6 months, leaving a widow and four sons. The following is his epitaph :—

Consigned to earth, here rests the lifeless clay,
  Which once a vital spark from Heaven inspired!
The lamp of genius shone full bright as day,
  Then left the world to mourn its light retired.
While beams that splendid orb which lights the spheres,
  While mountain streams descend to swell the main,
While changeful seasons mark the rolling years—
  Thy fame, O BURNS, let Scotia still retain.

68. From Barton Stacey Churchyard, Hants. On MR. JOHN COLLINCE :—

Where 'twas I liv'd or dy'd, it matters not;
To whom related, or by whom begot;

I was, but am not; ask no more of me ;
It's all I am, and all that you must be.

69. On a Country Sexton :—

He that carried many a body brave,
Was carried by a fever to the grave ;
He carried, and was carried ; that's even :
Lord! make him Porter to the gates of Heaven!

70. From Bishop Cumming's Churchyard, Wilts :—

At my right hand lies my son JOHN,
 As we did lay in bed ;
And there do lay till Christ do say,
 "Come out ye dead."

71. On a Famous Boxer :—

Death took him in the UPPER VIEW,
 And gave him such a BRACE ;
The grapple turn'd him black and blue,
 And made him shift his place.
PARTS OF ACCESS he next assailed,
 With such a KNOCK-DOWN BLOW
As never yet to mortals fail'd
 A total overthrow.

72. On the Wife of Dr. Greenwood.

Mrs. Greenwood was buried in Southampton Churchyard, the following very singular lines having been written upon her by her husband:—

O cruel Death! thou hast cut down
The fairest Green-wood in all this kingdom.
Her virtue and her piety were such,
That really she deserved a Lord or a Judge:
Yet such was her humility,
That she rather chose me, a Doctor in Divinity;
For which heroic action, join'd to all the rest,
She deserves to be esteemed the Phœnix of her sex;
And like that bird her young she did beget,
That those she left behind might not be disconsolate.
And now, my grief for this good woman is so sore,
That really I can write but four lines more.
For this and for another good woman's sake,
Never let a blister be applied to a lying-in woman's neck,
For in all diseases of the bladder and the womb,
It never fails to bring the patient to the tomb.
Dr. Greenwood *fecit*.

73. On John Baskerville.

Extract from the very singular will of the late

Mr. John Baskerville, a celebrated printer at Birmingham, who died in 1775,—together with his epitaph, written by himself:—

My farther will and pleasure is, and I do hereby declare, that the devise of my goods and chattels, as above, is upon the express condition, that my wife, in concert with my executors, do cause my body to be buried in a conical building in my own premises, heretofore used as a mill, which I have lately raised higher and painted, and in a vault, which I have prepared for it. This doubtless to many will appear *a whim;* perhaps it is so, but it is a whim for many years resolved upon, as I have a hearty contempt of all *superstition, the farce of a consecrated ground,* the Irish barbarism of "sure and certain hopes," etc. As I also consider *Revelation,* as it is called, exclusive of the *scraps of morality casually* intermixed with it, to be [we omit here a very indecent reflection]. I expect some shrewd remarks will be made on this my declaration by the *ignorant* and *bigoted,* who cannot distinguish between *religion* and *superstition,* and are taught the belief that *morality* (by which I understand all the duties a man owes to God and his fellow-creatures) is not sufficient to entitle him to Divine favour, without professing to believe (as they call it) certain *absurd doctrines* and *mysteries,* of which they have no more conceptions or ideas than a horse. This morality alone I profess to have been my religion, and the rule of my actions; to which I appeal how far my profession and practice has been consistent.

The *Epitaph*.

Stranger,
Beneath this cone, in *unconsecrated* ground,
A friend to the liberties of mankind directed his body to be inurned.
May the example contribute to emancipate thy mind
From the idle fears of Superstition,
And the wicked Arts of Priesthood!

74. On a Landlord :—

Hic Jacet WALTER GUN,
Sometime landlord of the Tun;
Sic transit gloria mundi!
He drank hard upon Friday,
That being a high day,
Then took to his bed and died upon Sunday!

75. From St. Botolph's, Aldersgate :—

Hic conjuncta suo recubat FRANCISCA marito;
Et cinis est unis; quæ fuit una caro,

Huc cineres conferre suos soror ANNA jubebat ;
  Corpore sic uno pulvere trina jacent.
Sic Opifex rerum Omnipotens ; qui, trinus et unus,
  Pulvere ab hoc uno corpora trina dabit.

Which may be rendered into English as follows :—

Close to her husband, FRANCES, join'd once more,
Lies here—ONE dust, which was ONE flesh before ;
Here, as enjoin'd, her sister ANNE'S remains
Were laid : ONE dust, three bodies thus contains.
Th' Almighty Source of things, the immense THREE-ONE,
Will raise THREE bodies from thy dust alone.

76. From Clevedon, Somersetshire.

The secluded village church of Clevedon, on the Bristol Channel, presented in January, 1859, a memorable and impressive scene, when the remains of the late HENRY HALLAM, the historian, were conveyed from Clevedon Court, the seat of Sir Arthur Hallam Elton, M.P., nephew of the deceased, to a grave which, through a mysterious inversion of the common order of succession, had been already rendered classic ground by the ashes of his two gifted sons. The funeral was strictly private, but it accomplished that pious wish so touchingly expressed in the epitaph written by himself over his eldest son :—

Vale,
Dulcissime, dilectissime, desideratissime,
Hic, posthac Pater ac Mater
Requiescamus Tecum
Usque ad Tuham.

77. On a Spendthrift :—

> Stop, passenger, for here is laid
> One who the debt of nature paid.
> This is not strange, the reader cries,
> We all know here a dead man lies.
> You're right; but stop, I'll tell you more :
> He never paid a debt before ;
> And now he's gone, I'll further say
> He never will another pay.

78. From Horsleydown Church, Cumberland.

The following is remarkable for its outspokenness :—

Here lie the bodies of THOMAS BOND, and MARY his wife. She was temperate, chaste, and charitable, but she was proud, peevish, and passionate. She was an affectionate wife and tender mother, but her husband and child, whom she loved, seldom saw her countenance without a disgusting frown—while she received visitors whom she despised with an enduring smile. Her behaviour was discreet towards strangers, but imprudent in her family. Abroad her conduct was influenced by good breeding, but at home by ill-temper.

And so the epitaph runs on to a considerable length, acknowledging the good qualities of the poor woman, but killing each by setting against it some peculiarly remarkable trait. We confess that our feeling is quite turned in her favour by the unmanly assault which is made upon her by her brother, who is the author of the epitaph.

79. From Marnhull Churchyard:—

>I in great haste was snatched away,
>Scarce having time to read or pray.
>Read as a warning with me to try
>And always be prepared to die.

80. By Robert Herrick on BEN JONSON, who was born in 1574 and died in 1637.

> Here lies JONSON with the rest
> Of the poets, but the best.
> Reader, would'st thou more have known?
> Ask his story, not the stone;
> That will speak what this can't tell
> Of his glory; so farewell!

81. From a Scotch Graveyard :—

> Here lies interr'd a man o' micht,
> His name was MALCOLM DOWNIE;
> He lost his life, ae market nicht,
>   By fa'in' off his pownie.

82. By Dr. Goldsmith, on THOMAS PARNELL, the Poet: born in 1679; died, 1717.

> This tomb, inscribed to gentle PARNELL'S name,
> May speak our gratitude, but not his fame.
> What art but feels his sweetly moral lay,
> That leads to truth through pleasure's flow'ry way?
> Celestial themes confess'd his tuneful aid;
> And heaven, that lent him genius, was repaid.
> Needless to him the tribute we bestow,
> The transitory breath of fame below;

More lasting rapture from his works shall rise,
While converts thank their poet in the skies.

83. By Robert Burns, on ROBERT FERGUSSON the Poet: born 1751; died 1774.

> No sculptur'd marble here, nor pompous lay!
> No storied urn, nor animated bust!
> This simple stone directs pale Scotia's way
> To pour her sorrows o'er the poet's dust.

84. From Eton College.

The following is to be seen on an oblong brass plate, in Lupton's Chapel, Eton College :—

> Ano: 1372. August 18 daye.
> Under this stone lies Thomas Smith, late a fellow heare,
> And of Cambridge, a Master of Arte of ye King Colledge theare.
> He did depart from earthly life, the time above exprest,
> Whose soule we hope dothe now remaine in Abram's brest.

85. On Sir HENRY WOTTON.

In the same place (Eton) Sir Henry Wotton

has the following curious epitaph, in the Latin language, inscribed above his grave :—

> Here lies the author of this sentence :
> *An itching for dispute is the scab of the church.*
> Seek his name elsewhere.

86. By Douglas Jerrold on CHARLES KNIGHT.

After an evening of friendly talk with a party which included the late Douglas Jerrold and Charles Knight, between whom a close friendship had subsisted for many years, they walked homewards together. In the course of the evening the conversation had turned upon epitaphs, and Knight, half in jest, half in earnest, had asked the great wit to write his epitaph for him. The incident had escaped Knight's recollection, but on arriving at the point where they were to part each for his own house, it was recalled to his memory by Jerrold himself. "I've got the epitaph for you," said he. " Well, what is it ? "

"Good KNIGHT!"

And with that they parted.

87. From St. John's Churchyard, Devizes:—

> Life's uncertain—Death is sure,
> Sin is the wound—Christ's the cure.

Likewise in Llandovery and other churchyards.

88. From St. Mary's Churchyard, York.

On a young woman who was accidentally drowned, December 24th, 1696. The inscription is said to have been penned by her lover :—

> Nigh to the River Ouse, in York's fair city,
> Unto this pretty maid Death shewed no pity;
> As soon as she'd her pail of water fill'd,
> Came sudden Death, and Life, like water, spill'd.

89. On a Yorkshire Cook:—

> Underneath this crust
> Lies the mouldering dust
> Of ELEANOR BATCHELOR SHOVEN,
> Well versed in the Arts
> Of pies, custards, and tarts,
> And the lucrative trade of the oven.
> When she lived long enough
> She made her last puff,

A puff by her husband much praised,
   And now she doth lie
   And make a dirt pie,
In hopes that her crust may be raised.

90. On Mr. Pat Steel :—

   Here lies PAT STEEL,
     That's very true.
   Who was he ? What was he ?
     What is that to you ?

91. On William Llewellyn, the Learned Collier of Mangotsfield, in Gloucestershire :—

Beneath this humble turf there lies
An honest collier, learn'd and wise ;
His mind, by love of knowledge fired,
To wisdom more than wealth aspired ;
And thought it was a happy lot
To dwell with knowledge in a cot.
To latest life from early youth
His search was philosophic truth ;
And oft from nightly rest he stole
To seek the charmer of his soul.
In Nature's book, by nature taught,
He learned to think as Newton thought ;

And with an astronomic eye
Measured the rolling orbs on high.
He knew the courses, motions, reign,
Of all the planetary train,
And with precision just and clear
Marked out the order of the year.
To him were nature's treasures known,
And science made them all his own.
What though not wealth, nor honoured birth
Distinguished him for men of earth—
What though no state nor letter'd name
Enrolled him in the list of fame—
His soul aspired to nobler things,
And left the world to lords and kings!
Content to enjoy the better part,
A knowing head and honest heart.
Accept, O sage, the tribute due,
   To worth so simply great as thine;
And let the learn'd with candour view
   What friendship offers at this shrine.

92. From Churchill.

In the church at Churchill, on the north side of the chancel, is a quaint monument, which, according to tradition, is an effigy of SIR JOHN

Latch (1644), dressed in a coat of buff, boots, and spurs, looking on his wife in a shroud; beneath, on the front of the tomb, are seven boys and four girls kneeling on cushions. On the monument is the following quaint but beautiful inscription, said to have been written by the celebrated Dr. Donne :—

> Living and dead, thou seest how here we lie,
> I dote on death, preparing how to die.
> Ah, fleeting life! she is gone. Aye, summons me
> Unto the grave, so will posterity;
> Though singling death the sacred knot undo,
> By parting two make one once more in two;
> I see 'tis, Lord, by Thy Divine decree,
> Thus one by one to take us home to Thee;
> Whose risen Christ doth us assurance give,
> He'll rouse this grave, and we with Him shall live;
> He rich in grace, though poor in stable cratch—
> So have ye here—here laid up, SARAH LATCH.

93. From the Church of St. Mary, Wedmore.

In this church, on an ancient monumental tablet, may be seen the following inscription :—

Sacred to the memorie of CAPTAIN THOMAS HODGES, of the county of Somerset, esq.; who at the siege of Antwerpe, about 1583, with unconquered courage, wonne two ensignes from the enemy, where, receiving his last wound, he gave three legacies: his soule to the Lord Jesus, his body to be lodged in Flemish earth, his heart to be sent to his dear wife in England :—

>   Here lies his wounded heart, for whome
>   One kingdom was too small a roome:
>   Two kingdoms therefore have thought good to part
>   So stout a body and so brave a heart.

94. From the Churchyard of Cherening-le-Clay, Dorsetshire.

A sorrowful husband, after recording the death of his beloved wife, ANN HUGHES, ends in the following ridiculous manner :—

>   Who far below this tomb doth rest,
>   Has join'd the army of the blest.
>   The Lord has ta'en her to the sky:
>   The saints rejoice, *and so do I.*

95. From Bristol Cathedral.

On the monument of MRS. MASON, wife of

the Rev. William Mason, the distinguished Poet —1767:—

 Take, holy earth, all that my soul holds dear;
  Take that best gift, which Heav'n so lately gave.
 To Bristol's fount I bore, with trembling tear,
  Her faded form; she bowed to taste the wave,
 And died! Does youth, does beauty read the line?
  Does sympathetic fear their breast alarm?
 Speak, dead Maria! breathe a strain divine—
  E'en from the grave thou shalt have power to charm.
 Bid them be chaste, be innocent like thee;
  Bid them in duty's sphere as meekly move;
 And if so fair, from vanity as free,
  As firm in friendship, and as fond in love,
 Tell them, though 'tis an awful thing to die
  ('Twas e'en to thee), yet, the dead path once trod,
 Heav'n lifts her everlasting portals high,
  And bids the pure in heart behold their GOD!

96. From Anglesey Churchyard, 1740:—

  Who in the grave or silent Dust
   Our bodyes scattered lyes,
  We trust in God at the last Day
   In glory we shall rise.

97. From Barrow-upon-Soar, Leicestershire.

This churchyard contains a very punning epitaph on one CAVE :—

> Here in this grave there lies a CAVE :
> We call a cave a grave.
> If cave be grave, and grave be Cave,
> Then reader, judge, I crave,
> Whether doth Cave lie here in grave
> Or grave here lie in Cave :
> If grave in Cave here buried lie,
> Then, grave, where is thy victory?
> Go, reader, and report here lies a Cave,
> Who conquers death, and buries his own grave.

98. From Arlington Churchyard, Devonshire :—

> Here lies WILL BURGOIN, a Squire by descent,
> Whose death in this world many people lament:
> The rich for his love,
> The poor for his alms,
> The wise for his knowledge,
> The sick for his balms.
> Grace he did love, and vice control ;
> Earth hath his body, and heaven his soul.
> The twelfth day of August in the morn died he,
> 1 6 2 and 3.

99. As true as it is truly Popish.

The following is inscribed upon a monument in one of the Catholic Chapels in the city of Cork :—

I. H. S. Sacred to the memory of the benevolent EDWARD MOLLOY, the friend of humanity and the father of the poor. He employed the wealth of this world only to secure the riches of the next; and leaving a balance of merit on the book of life, he made heaven debtor to his mercy. He died Oct. 17th, 1818, aged ninety. R. I. P.

100. From Upton-on-Severn, Gloucestershire :—

> Beneath this stone, in hopes of Zion,
> Doth lie the landlord of the Lion;
> His son keeps on the business still,
> Resigned unto the heavenly will.

As an advertisement this is pretty good, but the American epitaph (No. 101), on Mrs. Smith, does the advertising business more effectually.

101. An American Epitaph :—

Here lies JANE SMITH, wife of Thomas Smith, marble-cutter: this monument was erected by her husband as a tribute to her memory and a specimen of his work. Monuments of the same style, 250 dollars.

Better still, however, will that be on James Gordon Bennett (No. 102). The present proprietor of the *New York Herald* is about to erect a monument over his father's grave at a cost of £50,000—in doing which he advertises his paper most effectually.

102. On JAMES GORDON BENNETT :—

>JAMES GORDON BENNETT,
>aged seventy-two,
>founder of the *New York Herald.*

103. Political Epitaph. Here we have another version of No. 55 :—

>Here lies NED HYDE,
>Because he died ;
>If it had been his sister,
>We should have missed her ;
>But we would rather
>It had been his father ;

Or, for the good of the nation,
The whole generation.

104. On Copernicus, St. Anne's Church, Cracow :—

Sta, sol, ne moveare.
(*Stand, O sun, move not.*)

105. From Melrose Church :—

Earth builds on earth castles and towers ;
Earth says to earth, all shall be ours ;
Earth walks on earth all clad in gold ;
Earth goes to earth sooner than earth wold.

106. On DR. FRANKLIN, by himself :—

The body of BENJAMIN FRANKLIN, printer (like the cover of an old book, its contents torn out, and stripped of its lettering and gilding), lies here, food for worms ; yet the work itself will not be lost, for it will (as he believed) appear once more in a new and more beautiful edition, corrected and amended by the Author.

107. From Cameley Churchyard, Somersetshire :—

If love and care could death prevent,
Our days had not so soon been spent.

> Life was desired, but God did see
> Eternal life was best for me.

108. From Babington Churchyard, Somersetshire :—

> Prepare to follow, for be sure
> thou must
> One day, as well as I, be
> turned to Dust.

109. Fonetik Eppetaff. From a stone in Lansdown Cemetery, Bath :—

> In memori ov
> MERI PITMAN,
> Weif ov Mr. Eizak Pitman,
> Fonetik Printer, ov this Siti.
> Deid 19 Agust 1857, edjed 64.
> " Preper tu mit thei God."
> Emos 4—12.

110. A blundering one, from St. Andrew's, Plymouth :—

Here lies the body of JAMES VERNOR, Esq., only *surviving* son of Admiral Vernor : died the 23rd July, 1753.

111. A blundering one, from Karl Keel:

Here lie the remains of THOMAS NICHOLS, who died in Philadelphia, March, 1753. *Had he lived he would have been buried here.*

112. A blundering one, from Montrose, 1757:—

Here lyes the bodeys of GEORGE YOUNG and all their *posterity* for more than fifty years backwards.

113. From a Churchyard near Thornton, Yorkshire:—

> Here lies the body of JOHN TROLLOPE,
> Whose hands made these stones to roll up;
> When God Almighty took his soul up,
> His body went to fill the hole up.

114. From St. Mary Redcliff, Bristol:—

MR. WILLIAM CANING'S ye Richest Marchant of ye towne of Bristow. Afterwards chosen 5 times Mayor of ye said town for ye good of ye Comen Wealth of y same. Hee was in order of priesthood 7 yeares, and afterwards Deane of Westbury, and died ye 7th of Novem. 1474, which said William did build within ye said towne of Westbury a College (which his Canons) and yᵉ said William did maintain by space of 8 yeares: 800 handy craftsmen, besides carpenters and masons every day: 100 men. Besides King Edward yᵉ 4th had of yᵉ said William 3000 marks for his peace to be had in 2470 tonnes of shiping; these are yᵉ names of his shiping with their burthens:—

	tonnes.		tonnes.
Yᵉ Mary Caning	400	Yᵉ Mary Balt	220
Yᵉ Mary Redcliff	500	Yᵉ Little Nicholas	140
Yᵉ Mary and John	900	Yᵉ Margaret	220
Yᵉ Galliott	050	Yᵉ Katherine of Bolt	122
Yᵉ Katherine	140	A Ship in Ireland	100

No age nor time can wear out well woon fame,
    The stones themselves a flatly worke doth shew.
From senceless grave we ground may man's good name,
    And noble minds by vent'rous acts we know.
A Lanterne cleere settes forth a candle light,
    A worthy act declares a worthy might.
The buildings rare that here you may behold
    To shrine his Bones deserves a tomb of gold;
The famous Fabric that he here hath donne
    Shines in its sphere as glorious as the sonne.
What needes more words? yᵉ future world he sought,
And set yᵉ pompe and pride of this at nought.
    Heaven was his ame, let heaven be still his station
That leaves such work *for others' imitation.*

115. From St. Giles' Churchyard, Northampton :—

Here lies a most dutiful daughter, honest and just,
Awaiting the resurrection in hopes to be one of the first.

116. On a Cardinal :—

> Here lies a Cardinal, who wrought
> Both good and evil in his time;
> The good he did was good for nought;
> Not so the evil! that was prime.

117. From a Churchyard in Staffordshire :—

> This turf has drank a
> widow's tear;
> Three of her husbands
> slumber here.

It may be interesting to note that the tearful widow was still living with a fourth partner.

118. By Walter Savage Landor. For the grave of Mr. G. P. R. JAMES, at Venice :—

GEORGE PAYNE RAINSFORD JAMES, British Consul-General in the Adriatic, died at Venice, aged 60, on the

9th of June, 1860. His merits as a writer are known wherever the English language is, and as a man they rest on the hearts of many. A few friends have erected this humble and perishable monument.

119. From the Churchyard of Allowa. On the Rev. ROBERT JOHNSTON, parish minister of that place :—

> Before this monument of stones
> Lie honest ROBERT JOHNSTON'S bones;
> He lived devoutly, died in peace ;
> Prompt by religion and grace,
> Endowed a preacher for this place.
> With consent of his wife to be
> Here by him when she falls to dee.
> At her expense this tomb was raised
> For him whose worth she prized and praised.

120. On an Infant :—

> Bold infidel, lie down and die.
> Beneath this stone an Infant's ashes lie ;
> Say, is he lost or saved ?
> If death's by sin, he died because he's here ;
> If Heaven's by works, in Heaven he can't appear.

Revere the Bible's sacred page, the knot's untied :
He died, for Adam sinn'd—he lives, for Jesus died.

121. From St. John's Church, Beverley, Yorkshire.

On the outside is an oval stone tablet; on the upper portion are sculptured two straight swords, crossed, painted and gilded, beneath which are the following lines :—

> Here two young Danish Souldiers lye :
> The one in quarrell chanced to die;
> The other's Head, by their own Law,
> With Sword was severed at one Blow.
> December the 23rd, 1692.

122. From Jersey :—

> Here lies JOHN ROSS,
> Kicked by a Hoss.

123. From St. Albans Abbey :—

In memory of THOMAS SHEPPARD, son of Thomas and Mary Sheppard. Died February 15th, 1766, aged 30 years :—

Great was my grief, I could not rest;
God called me hence,—He thought it best;
Unhappy marriage was my fate,
I did repent when it was too late.

124. From Arlington, near Paris:—

Two grandmothers with their two granddaughters,
Two husbands with their two wives,
Two fathers with their two daughters,
Two mothers with their two sons,
Two maidens with their two mothers,
Two sisters with their two brothers,
Yet but six corps in all, lie buried here,
All born legitimate, from incest clear.

125. On a Tippler:—

The young gentleman referred to here
Killed himself by drinking October beer.
  Here lie I must
  Wrapp'd up in dust,
   Confinèd to be sober.
  Clarke, take care,
  Lest you come here,
   For faith here's no October.

126. On Dr. Bentley:—

    Visitors tread gently,
    Here lies Dr. Bentley.

127. On a Virtuous Wife:—

    Behold this grave, it doth embrace
    A virtuous wife, with *Rachel's* comely face,
    Sarah's obedience, *Lydia's* open heart,
    Martha's care, and *Mary's* better part.

128. From St. Bennet's, Paul's Wharf, London:—

Here lies one More, and no *More* than he.
One *More*, and no *More!* how can that be?
Why one *More* and no *More* may well lie here alone:
But here lies one *More*, and that's *More* than one.

129. From Newington Churchyard:—

    Life's but a jest,
    And all things show it;
    I thought so once,
    But now I know it.

130. From Newbury Churchyard:—

Here lays John, with Mary his bride,—

They lived and they laugh'd while they was able,
And at last was obliged to knock under the table.

131. By a French Husband:—

    Here lies my wife,
      A fact that must tell
    For her repose,
      And for mine as well.

132. From Venice:—

JOANNI MAGIO,
Puero incomparabili,
Qui, ob imperitiam obstetricis,
Ex utero statim translatus
Est at tumulum, die 21 Decemb.
MDXXXII.

[*Translation.*]
To the memory of JOHN MAGHI,
An incomparable boy,
Who, through the unskilfulness of the midwife,
on the 21st day of December, 1532,
was translated from the womb to the tomb.

133. From St. Mary's Churchyard, Hereford:—

Here lieth old BECK, who sold fruit at the cross,
And now she's departed, we shall have a loss;

She was a good wife, and a kind loving mother,
And, all things considered, we've scarce such another.

134. From Ripon Cathedral :—

Here lyeth JOHN JAMES, the old cook of Newby, whc was a faithful servant to his master, and an upright downright honest man :—

> Banes among stanes
> Do lie sou still,
> Whilk the soul wanders
> E'en where God will.

135. On a Bad Violinist :—

> When Orpheus played he moved Old Nick :
> But thou only moved thy fiddle-stick.

We have another on a fiddler, see No. 192.

136. From Norwich Cathedral :—

> Here lies the body of honest TOM PAGE,
> Who died in the 33rd year of his age.

137. From Aberconway Churchyard, Caernarvonshire :—

Here lieth the body of NICHOLAS HOOKS, of Conway,

gent., who was the *one-and-fortieth child* of his father, William Hooks, Esq., by Alice his wife, and *the father of seven-and-twenty children;* he died the 20th day of March, 1637.

138. At Nettlebed, Oxfordshire :—

> Here lies Father and Mother, and Sister and I,
> Wee all died within the space of one short year ;
> They be all buried at Wimble, except I,
> And I be buried here.

139. From an old source :—

> Whoso him bethought,
> Inwardly and oft,
> How sore it were to flit
> From life into the pit,
> From pit into pain
> Which ne'er shall cease again,
> He would not do one sin,
> All the world to win.

140. On a Child :—

> This little hero that lies here,
> Was conquered by the diarrheer.

141. On JOHN BUNN :—

>Here lies JOHN BUNN,
>Who was killed by a gun.

His name wasn't Bunn, but his real name was Wood,
But Wood wouldn't rhyme with gun, so I thought Bu should.

142. On JOHN MACPHERSON :—

>JOHN MACPHERSON was a remarkable person :
>He stood 6 feet 2 without his shoe,
>And he was slew at Waterloo.

143. On MRS. STOKES :—

>Here lies the wife of SIMON STOKES,
>Who lived and died—like other folks.

144. On MRS. STONE :—

>Curious enough, we all must say,
>That what was STONE should now be clay :
>More curious still, to own we must,
>That what was Stone will soon be dust.

145. From Whittlesea Churchyard, Ely :—

>Here lieth the body of ELIZABETH
>ADDISON—John, her son,
>And Old Roger to come.

146. On an Infant eight months old :—

> Since I have been so quickly done for,
> I wonder what I was begun for.

147. From Bury St. Edmunds, Suffolk :—

> Here lies JANE KITCHEN,
> Who when her glass was spent,
> She kickt up her heels,
> And away she went.

A similar epitaph is said likewise to be at Winchester.

148. On ROGER NORTON :—

> Here lies, alas! poor ROGER NORTON,
> Whose sudden death was oddly brought on!
> Trying one day his corns to mow off,
> The razor slipped and cut his toe off!
> The toe, or rather what it grew to,
> An inflammation quickly flew to;
> The part then took to mortifying,
> Which was the cause of Roger's dying.

149. An icy one.

A curious record of an accident, occasioned by

the downfall of ice, is to be found as an epitaph on the son of the then parish clerk at Bampton, in Devonshire, who was killed by an icicle falling upon and fracturing his skull:

> In memory of the Clerk's son:—
> Bless my i, i, i, i, i, i,
> Here I lies,
> In a sad pickle,
> Killed by icicle.

150. On HOGARTH,

Who lies in a superb tomb, with his wife, the daughter of Sir James Thornhill, and her mother, in Chiswick Churchyard. Garrick wrote the following lines, which are still visible:—

> Farewell, great painter of mankind,
>   Who reach'd the noblest point of art;
> Whose pictured morals charm the mind,
>   And, through the eye, correct the heart.
> If genius fire thee, reader, stay;
>   If nature touch thee, drop a tear;
> If neither move thee, turn away,
>   For Hogarth's honour'd dust lies here.

151. From Belturbet Churchyard, Ireland:—

Here lies JOHN HIGLEY, whose father and mother were drowned in their passage from America. Had they both lived they would have been buried here.

152. On CHRISTOPHER THUMB, at Frome, Somerset:—

> Stretch'd underneath this stone is laid
> Our neighbour GOODMAN THUMB;
> We trust, although full low his head,
> He'll rise i' the world to come.
> This humble monument will show
> Where lies an honest man.
> Ye kings whose heads are laid as low,
> Rise higher if ye can.

153. From Hyden Churchyard, Yorkshire:—

Here lies the body of WILLIAM STRATTON, of Paddington, buried 18th day of May, 1734, aged 97 years; who had by his first wife 28 children; by his second 17; was own father to 45; grandfather to 86; great-grandfather to 23. In all 154 children.

154. On JOHN HILL:—

Here lies JOHN HILL,
A man of skill,
Whose age was five times ten :
He never did good,
And never would,
If he'd lived as long again.

155. A simple one :—

Poor
Simple thing,
He,
Nought suspecting,
Meant to be blessed,
but,
found himself undone.

156. From Everton. Written, excepting the date of his death, by himself :—

Here lie
The earthly remains of
JOHN BERRIDGE,
Late Vicar of Everton,
And an Itinerant Servant of Jesus Christ,
Who loved his Master and His work,
And after running on His errands many years,

Was caught up to wait on Him above.
Reader,
Art thou born again?
No salvation without a new birth.
I was born in sin February, 1716;
Remained ignorant of my fallen state till 1730,
Lived proudly on faith and works for
salvation till 1754;
Admitted to Everton vicarage 1755;
Fled to Jesus alone for refuge 1756;
Fell asleep in Christ January 22, 1793.

157. An epigrammatic one:—

This corpse
Is Tommy Thorpe's.

[*Revised edition.*]
Thorpe's
Corpse.

158. A queer one. From a Graveyard at Baton Rouge, La:—

Here lies buried in this tomb
A constant sufferer from salt rheum,
Which finally in truth did pass
To spotted erysipelas.

A husband brave, a father true,
Here he lies, and so must you.

159. On a gold-digger.

The following was taken from a head-board at a grave in the Sparta Diggings, California; and, taking the orthography into consideration, it is an apparently unconscious blending of the serio-comic with the would-be sublime :—

In memory ov
JOHN SMITH, who met
wierlent death neer this spot,
18 hundred and 40 too. He was shot
by his own pistill;
It was not one of the new kind,
but a old fashioned
brass barrel, and of such is the
Kingdom of heaven.

160. On a Wife.

A man in New Hampshire had the misfortune recently to lose his wife. Over the grave he caused a stone to be placed, on which, in the depth of his grief, he had ordered to be inscribed :—

    Tears cannot restore her—therefore I weep.

161. The briefest Epitaph on record. On a Fellow of the Oxford University :—

    Præivit.
    (*He is gone before.*)

162. On the Author of "Jerusalem Delivered":—

    Ossa TASSI.
    (*The bones of* TASSO.)

For brevity we may likewise note that on Ben Jonson.

163. From the Poet's Corner, Westminster Abbey:—

    Oh, rare BEN JONSON!

164. On GEORGE FREDERICK COOK, the great tragedian, in St. Paul's, New York:—

    Three kingdoms claim his birth ;
    Two hemispheres proclaim his worth.

165. On an English Baronet, in the time of Henry the Third:—

> All Christian men in my behalf,
> Pray for the soul of SIR JOHN CALF.

166. On JOHN ROSEWELL, A.D. 1687:—

This grave's a bed of roses—here doth lie
JOHN ROSEWELL, gent.;—his wife nine children by.

167. From Wolstanton. On ANNE JENNINGS:—

> Some have children, some have none;
> Here lies the mother of twenty-one.

168. From Barrow Churchyard. On MR. STONE:—

> Jerusalem's curse is not fulfilled in me,
> For here a *stone* upon a STONE you see.

169. On JOHN WHITE, in the Temple Church, London:—

Here lies JOHN, a burning, shining light,
Whose name, life, actions, all alike were WHITE.

170. On DR. POTTER, Archbishop of Canterbury, A.D. 1736:—

> Alack and well a-day!
> POTTER himself is turned to *clay*.

171. From Westminster Abbey. On JOHN GAY, the Poet, said to have been written by himself:—

> Life is a jest, and all things show it;
> I thought so once, but now I know it.

172. By the Poet DRYDEN, on the tomb of his wife:—

> Here lies my wife, here let her lie;
> She's now at rest, and so am I.

173. On REBECCA FREELAND, who died in the year 1741:—

> She drank good ale, good punch and wine,
> And lived to the age of ninety-nine.

174. On SIR CHRISTOPHER WREN:—

> Si monumentum quæris, circumspice.
> (*If his monument you seek, look around.*)

This is to be seen in St. Paul's, London, of

which, as is well known, Sir Christopher was the architect.

175. On a Wesleyan Minister.

The friends of Methodism may be pleased to read the following lines, which are copied from the plain slab which covers the dust of the REV. R. BOARDMAN, Wesleyan minister, at the Cathedral Church of Cork :—

<blockquote>
RICHARD BOARDMAN,
Departed this life Oct. 4th, 1782.
Ætatis 44.

Beneath this stone the dust of BOARDMAN lies,
His precious soul has soared above the skies.
With eloquence divine he preached the Word
To multitudes, and turned them to the Lord.
His bright example strengthened what he taught,
And devils trembled when for Christ he fought.
With truly Christian zeal he nations fired,
And all who knew him mourned when he expired.
</blockquote>

176. From South Wales.

In Vaynor Churchyard, near Merthyr Tydfil, not unlike the Irish epitaph, No. 34 :—

> Here lies the bodies of three
> Children dear,
> Two at Llanwono and
> One here.

(See No. 299.)

177. From a Churchyard in Pembrokeshire:—
> Here lie I, and no wonder I'm dead,
> For the wheel of the waggon went over my head.

178. From Curmwallon Churchyard, Cornwall:—
> Shall we all die?
> We shall die all.
> All die shall we?
> Die all we shall.

179. On a Collier:—
> Altho' his face was dirty,
>   His heart, they say, was clean.
> His age was only forty
>   When he ceased to have a being,—
> That is, he ceased to live,
>   So far as this world goes;
> But in the world above he wears
>   Perhaps a crown—who knows?

W. F.

180. On a Rich Man :—

>A man of wealth and fame,
>   Of honour and of worth;
>How powerful was his name
>   When living on the earth.
>But now he's left the world,
>   Where riches draw a line
>Distinguishing a man
>   From others of his kine.
>What now can this man do
>   With what he had whilst here?
>Not aught, for what he had—
>   In heaven it can't appear.
>We speak of him " in heaven,"
>   Well, let us hope he's there;
>Though the chances of such men
>   To get there are but rare.

181. On Husband and Wife.

The following is copied from a country churchyard :—

Here lies the body of JAMES ROBINSON, and RUTH his wife.

And underneath this text :—

> " Their warfare is accomplished."

182. From Torryburn Churchyard :—

> In this churchyard lies EPPIE COUTTS.
> Either here or hereabouts ;
> But whaur it is none can tell
> Till Eppie rise and tell hersel'.

183. From Oldbury-on-Severn :—

> Pain was my portion ;
> Physic was my food ;
> Groans my devotion ;
> Drugs did me no good.

184. On ROBERT BARRAS :—

> Poems and epitaphs are but stuff,
> Here lies BOB BARRAS, and that's enough.

185. From Broom Churchyard :—

> God be praised :
> Here is MR. DUDLEY, senior,
> And JANE his wife also,
> Who, while living was his superior,
> But see what death can do.
> Two of his sons also lie here,
> One WALTER, t'other JOE.
> They all of them went in the year
> 1510 below.

186. On two Brothers :—

Here lies two brothers by misfortune surrounded,
One died of his wounds and the other was drownded.

187. On Susan Mum :—

To the memory of Susan Mum :—
Silence is wisdom.

188. On William Beck :—

Here lies the body of William Beck,
He was thrown at a hunt and broke his neck.

189. From St. Mary's, Swansea. On Elizabeth, the wife of William Vidall, who died June 29th, 1843, aged 48 years :—

She was, but words are wanting to say what ;
Think what a wife should be—and she was that.

(See No. 4.)

190. From St. Mary's, Swansea. On Evan Harris :—

All you that see where I do lie,
As you are now, so once was I.

As I am now, so you shall be,
Cut down by death, and follow me.

(Similar to No. 14.)

191. On ROBERT GRAY, Taunton Church :—

Taunton bore him, London bred him ;
Piety trained him, virtue led him ;
Earth enrich'd, Heaven caress'd him ;
This thankful town, *that* mindful city,
Share his piety and his pity.
What he gave, and how he gave it,
Ask the poor, and you shall have it.
Gentle reader, Heaven may strike
Thy tender heart to do the like.
And now thy eyes have read this story,
Give him the praise, and Heaven the glory.

192. On a Fiddler named STEPHEN :—

STEPHEN and Time are now both even ;
Stephen beat Time, but now Time's beat Stephen.

193. From Shoreditch Churchyard :

We must all die, there is no doubt ;
Your glass is running—mine is out.

194. From Whitby Churchyard :—

> Sudden and unexpected was the end
> Of our esteemèd and belovèd friend ;
> He gave to all his friends a sudden shock,
> By one day falling into Sunderland Dock.

195. From St. Mary's, Swansea. On a child 3 months old :—

> Beneath this stone an infant lies,
> To earth whose body's lent,
> Which shall more pure hereafter rise,
> But not more innocent.
> When the last dreadful trump shall blow,
> And Souls to Bodies join,
> Millions will wish their lives below
> Had been as short as thine.
> O Sexton, do not with thy Death-like spade,
> Remove this earth where innocence is laid.

196. From the same place. On the wife of JOHN PROSSER :—

> ———Reader, pause,
> And think what a wife should be, and she was that!!

(See Nos. 4 and 189.)

197. On an Angler:—

    Hook'd it.

198. From St. Mary's, Swansea. On Hugh Somerville Head, R.N., aged 36 years:—

    When I am dead
    Let not the day be writ;
    Some will remember it ! ! !
    Deep let it rest
    In one fond female breast,
    Then is my memory blest.

199. On an Englishman troubled with *ennui*:—

Here lies Sir John Plumpudding, of the Grange,
Who hanged himself one morning for a change.

200. By Dr. Goldsmith, on Mr. Edwd. Pardon:—

    Here lies poor Ned Pardon, from misery freed,
      Who long was a bookseller's hack;
    He led such a damnable life in this world,
      I don't think he'll ever come back.

201. On Count Tessin.

On the tomb of Count Tessin, Governor of Gustavus III. of Sweden, written by himself:—

> Tandem felix.
> (*Happy at last.*)

202. On a Miser, by W. F.:—

> Gone underground.

203. On Sir Isaac Newton.

The following was intended for Newton's monument:—

> .Nature and nature's law lay hid in night;
> God said, *Let Newton be*—and all was light.

The epitaph on Sir Isaac, however, runs as follows:—

> Isaacum Newton
> Quem immortalem
> Testantur Tempus, Natura, Cœlum,
> Mortalum hoc marmor
> Fatetur.

(This marble acknowledges Isaac Newton mortal whom time, nature, and heaven prove immortal.)

204. On Pope Adrian.

His Holiness wrote the following sad epitaph for himself:—

> Adrianus Papa VI, hic situs est
> Qui nihil sibi infelicius
> In vita
> Quam quod imperaret
> Duxit.

Which may be rendered in English thus:—

Pope Adrian VI. lies here, who experienced nothing more unhappy in life than that he commanded.

205. By Pope, on Mrs. Corbett. This lady died of cancer in the breast:—

> Here rests a woman, good without pretence,
> Blest with plain reason and with sober sense.
> No conquests she, but o'er herself, desired,
> No arts essay'd, but not to be admired.
> Passion and pride were to her soul unknown,
> Convinc'd that virtue only is our own ;
> So unaffected, so composed a mind :
> So firm, yet soft, so strong, yet so refin'd ;
> Heaven as its purest gold, by tortures tried :
> The saint sustain'd it, but the woman died.

206. From the Unitarian Churchyard, Swansea:—

This humble stone, what few vain marbles can,
May safely say—here lies an honest man.

207. By Dr. Johnson on a Musician:—

PHILIPS, whose touch harmonious could remove
The pangs of guilty power and hopeless love,
Rest here, distressed by poverty no more;
Find here, that calm thou gav'st so oft before;
Sleep undisturbed within this peaceful shrine,
Till angels wake thee with a note like thine.

208. On a Smoker:—

My pipe's out.

209. From High Wycombe Churchyard.

The following lines are on MR. THOMAS ALDRIDGE, aged 90 years:—

Of no distemper,
Of no blast he died;
But fell
Like autumn fruit,
That's mellowed long,
E'en wondered at,
Because he dropt no sooner.

> Providence seemed to wind him up
> For fourscore years ; yet ran he on
> Nine winters more : till, like a clock,
> Worn out with beating time,
> The wheels of weary life
> At last stood still.

210. ON MATTHEW PRIOR.

The writer is not quite certain what Prior's epitaph is, but has thought that the following remarks may help his readers to form their own opinions :—

A writer in the *Quarterly Review* for January, 1865, says that Prior, who was most diligent in ransacking Greek, Latin, French, and English storehouses to come by his epigrams, in giving the epitaph for himself,—

> Gentlemen, here, by your leave,
>   Lie the bones of MATTHEW PRIOR,
> A son of Adam and Eve ;
>   Can Bourbon or Nassau go higher ?—

is only adopting a much older one by JOHN CARNEGIE :—

> JOHNNIE CARNEGIE lais heer,
>   Descendit of Adam and Eve;
> Gif ony can gang hicher,
> I'se willing gie him leve.

Touching this epitaph of Prior's, we give what is said in a review on "Familiar Words" by J. Hain Friswell, in the *Athenæum* for January 28th, 1865:—

"We will observe, too, that Mr. Friswell does wrong to Prior in seriously calling the following lines 'Prior's Epitaph on Himself':—

> "'Here lies what once was MATTHEW PRIOR,
>   The son of Adam and of Eve;
> Can Bourbon or Nassau claim higher?'

"This, of course," continues the reviewer (like Gay's heedless lines) "is a mere joke. Prior's lines, 'For my own Tombstone,' are in better taste:—

> "'To me 'twas giv'n to die; to thee 'tis giv'n
>   To live. Alas! one moment sets us ev'n.
>   Mark, how impartial is the Will of Heav'n!'"

According to *Chambers's Cyclopædia of Literature*, the following are the exact lines that were written by Prior :—

>Nobles and heralds, by your leave,
>>Here lies what once was MATTHEW PRIOR,
>
>The son of Adam and of Eve;
>>Can Stuart or Nassau claim higher?

210a. On THOMAS KEMP, who was hanged for sheep-stealing :—

>Here lies the body of THOMAS KEMP,
>Who lived by wool and died by hemp;
>There's nothing would suffice this glutton,
>But with the fleece to steal the mutton;
>Had he but worked and lived uprighter,
>He'd ne'er been hung for a sheep-biter.

211. From the Churchyard of Creltow, Salop :—

>On a Thursday she was born,
>On a Thursday made a bride,
>On a Thursday put to bed,
>On a Thursday broke her leg, and
>On a Thursday died.

In reading this epitaph I am reminded of an

old superstition about Friday being an unlucky day, and of a certain story told about a certain ship called *Friday*, built by a man who entertained no such foolish notions. I do not give the story, but now write an epitaph, which may be taken as strictly correct.

212. On the unlucky Ship "Friday":—

>On a Friday she was launched,
>On a Friday she set sail,
>On a Friday met a storm,
>And was lost, too, in the gale.

213. From Taibach Churchyard, South Wales:—

>Hurrah! my boys, at the Parson's fall,
>For if he'd lived he'd a-buried us all.

214. From Swaffham Churchyard, Norfolk:—

Here lies the body of THOMAS PARR;
What, old Tom? No! What, young Tom? Ah!

215. From Kensal Green Cemetery. Over the grave of MARGARET HARGRAVE, aged 31:—

'Tis ever thus, 'tis ever thus, with all that's best below,
The dearest, noblest, loveliest, are always first to go:
The bird that sings the sweetest, the pine that crowns the rock,
The glory of the garden, the flower of the flock.
'Tis ever thus, 'tis ever thus, with creatures heavenly fair:
Too finely formed to 'bide the storms more earthly natures bear,
A little while they dwell with us, blest ministers of love,
Then spread the wings we had not seen, and seek their home above.

216. From Maidstone Churchyard:—

> Here FRANCIS JARRATT lies—what then?
> Frank, when his Master calls, will rise again.

217. From Kensal Green. On E. B. BROWNING, aged 7 months:—

> The cup of life just to his lips he pressed,
> Found the taste bitter, and resigned the rest;
> Averse then turning from the face of day,
> He softly sighed his little soul away.

Note.—This epitaph, altered for a little girl, is

to be found in Prittlewell Churchyard, near Southend.

218. From St. George's, Southwark. On the young wife of a clergyman:—

> She came to the Cross when her young cheek was glowing,
> And raised to the Lord the bright glance of her eye;
> And when o'er her beauty death's darkness was flowing,
> Her God then upheld her; her Saviour was nigh.

219. From Morville Churchyard, near Bridgenorth. On JOHN CHARLTON, Esq.

He was for many years master of the Wheatland Foxhounds, and died January 20th, 1843, aged 63, regretted by all that knew him:—

> Of this world's pleasures I have had my share,
> And few the sorrows I was doomed to bear.
> How oft have I enjoyed the noble chase
> Of hounds and foxes, striving for the race;
> But, hark! the knell of death calls me away,
> Lo, sportsmen all, farewell! I must obey.

220. From Cambridge, on MARY GWYNNE :—

> Here lies the body of MARY GWYNNE,
> Who was so very pure within,
> She cracked the shell of her earthly skin,
> And hatched herself a cherubim.

221. An Epigrammatic one, from the Catacombs of Rome :—

> Hic VERUS qui semper vera locutus.

Which may be rendered thus :—

Here lies VERUS (truth), who always spoke truly.

221. On a Rich Man :—

> What I spent I had ; what I lent
> I lost ; what I gave I have.

222. From America :—

Died on the 11th inst., at his shop, No. 20, Greenwich Street, Mr. EDWARD JONES, much respected by all who knew and dealt with him. As a man he was amiable; as a hatter upright and moderate. His virtues were beyond all price, and his beaver hats were only three dollars each. He has left a widow to deplore his loss, and a large stock to be sold cheap, for the benefit of his family. He was snatched to the other world in the prime of life, just as he had concluded an extensive purchase of felt, which he got so cheap that his widow can supply hats at more reasonable rates than any house in the city. His disconsolate family will carry on business with punctuality.

223. From Brancepeth Churchyard, Durham.

On the tombstone of a celebrated Surgeon :—

>What I was once some may relate;
>What I am now is all men's fate;
>What I shall be none can explain
>Until He that callèd calls again.

224. From Hanwell Churchyard :—

>Beneath this stone I do intrust
>Are the remnants of her worthy dust:
>Farewell awhile, ye silent tomb,
>Until your husband calls for room.

225. On a Painter :—

>Here lies a *finished* artist.

226. On Mr. Miles. From Webley Churchyard, Yorkshire :—

> This tombstone is a Milestone ;
> Hah ! how so ?
> Because beneath lies Miles, who's
> Miles below.

227. From Selby Churchyard, Yorkshire :—

> Here lies the body of poor Frank Rowe,
> Parish clerk and gravestone cutter,
> And this is writ to let you know
> What Frank for others used to do
> Is now for Frank done by another.

228. On a Sailor :—

> I am grounded.

229. From Bruton Church :—

> Here lies a man by all good men esteemed,
> Because they proved him really what he seemed.

230. Anonymous :—

> Reader, pass on, ne'er waste your time
> On bad biography and bitter rhyme ;

For what I am this cumbrous clay ensures,
And what I was is no affair of yours.

231. From Cheltenham Churchyard:—

Here lies the body of MOLLY DICKIE, the wife of Hall Dickie, tailor:—

> Two Great physicians first
> My loving husband tried
> To cure my pain
> In vain;
> At last he got a third,
> And then I died.

232. On a man who was killed by a Pump:—

> Here lies JOHN ADAMS, who received a thump,
> Right on the forehead, from the parish pump,
> Which gave him the quietus in the end,
> For many doctors did his case attend.

233. From St. Bride's, near Bridgend:—

> Farewell, my dear and loving wife,
> My children, and my friends,
> I hope in heaven to see you all
> When all things have their ends.

234. From Portsmouth :—

Here lies JEMMY LITTLE, a carpenter industrious,
A very good-natured man, but somewhat blusterous.
When that his little wife his authority withstood,
He took a little stick and banged her as he would.
His wife now left alone, her loss does so deplore,
She wishes Jemmy back to bang her a little more;
For now he's dead and gone this fault appears so small,
A little thing would make her think it was no fault at all.

235. From the Burying-ground, of Concord, Massachusetts :—

God wills us free—man wills us slaves;
I will as God wills: God's will be done.
Here lies the body of
JOHN JACK,
A native of Africa, who died
March, 1773, aged about sixty years.
Though born in a land of slavery,
He was born free;
Though he lived in a land of liberty,
He lived a slave;
Till, by his honest, though stolen, labours,
He acquired the source of slavery,
Which gave him his freedom:

Though not long before
Death, the great Tyrant,
Gave him his final emancipation,
And put him on a footing with kings.
Though a slave to vice,
He practised those virtues
Without which kings are but slaves.

236. By Dr. Arbuthnot, on the infamous COL. CHANTRES :—

Here continueth to rot the body of FRANCIS CHANTRES, who, with an inflexible constancy and inimitable uniformity of life, persisted, in spite of age and infirmities, in the practice of every human vice excepting prodigality and hypocrisy: his insatiable avarice exempting him from the first, his matchless impudence from the second. Nor was he more singular in the undeviating pravity of his manners than successful in accumulating wealth. For without trade or profession, without trust of public money, and without bribe-worthy service, he acquired, or more properly created, a ministerial estate. He was the only person of his time who could cheat without the mask of honesty: retain his primeval meanness when possessed of ten thousand a year; and having daily deserved the gibbet for what he did, was at last condemned to it for what he could not do. Oh! indignant reader, think not his life useless to mankind. Providence connived at his execrable designs, to give to after ages a conspicuous proof and example of how small estimation is exorbitant wealth in the sight of God, by His bestowing it on the most unworthy of all mortals.

237. On JACK and JOAN, by Matthew Prior :—

> Interr'd beneath this marble stone
> Lie sauntering JACK and idle JOAN;
> While rolling threescore years and one
> Did round this globe their courses run ;
> If human things went ill or well,
> If changing empires rose or fell,
> The morning past, the evening came,
> And found this couple just the same.
> They walked and ate, good folks : what then ?
> Why, then they walked and ate again ;
> They soundly slept the night away,
> They did just nothing all the day ;
> Nor sister either had nor brother,
> They seem'd just tallied for each other.
> Their moral and economy
> Most perfectly they made agree ;
> Each virtue kept its proper bound,
> Nor trespass'd on the other's ground.

Nor fame nor censure they regarded,
They neither punished nor rewarded;
He cared not what the footman did;
Her maids she never prais'd nor chid:
So every servant took his course,
And bad at first, they all grew worse.
Slothful disorder filled his stable,
And sluttish plenty deck'd her table.
Their beer was strong, their wine was port,
Their meal was large, their grace was short.
They gave the poor the remnant meat,
Just when it grew not fit to eat.
They paid the church and parish rate,
And took, but read not, the receipt;
For which they claim'd their Sundays' due
Of slumbering in an upper pew.
No man's defects sought they to know,
So never made themselves a foe.
No man's good deeds did they commend,
So never rais'd themselves a friend.
Nor cherish'd they relations poor,
That might decrease their present store;
Nor barn nor house did they repair,
That might oblige their future heir.
They neither wanted nor abounded.
Nor tear nor smile did they employ
At news of public grief or joy.

When bells were rung and bonfires made,
If ask'd, they ne'er denied their aid.
Their jug was to the ringers carried,
Whoever either died or married.
Their billet at the fire was found,
Whoever was depos'd or crown'd.
Nor good, nor bad, nor fools, nor wise,
They would not learn, nor could advise ;
Without love, hatred, joy, or fear,
They led a kind of, as it were ;
Nor wish'd, nor car'd, nor laugh'd, nor cried,
And so they lived and so they died.

238. On an Accomplished Parish Officer, at Crayford, Kent :—

Here lieth the body of
PETER ISNELL
(30 years Clerk of this parish).

He lived respected as a pious and mirthful man, and died on his way to church to assist at a wedding on the 31st day of March, 1811, aged 70 years.

The inhabitants of Crayford have raised this stone to his cheerful memory, and as a tribute to his long and faithful services.

The life of this Clerk was just threescore and ten,
Nearly half of which time he had sung out *Amen*.

In his youth he was married, like other young men,
But his wife died one day, so he chanted *Amen.*
A second he took—she departed: what then?
He married and buried a third with *Amen.*
Thus his joys and his sorrows were *Trebled;* but then
His voice was deep Bass, as he sung out *Amen.*
On the *horn* he could blow as well as most men,
So his *horn* was exalted in blowing *Amen.*
But he lost all his *Wind* after threescore and ten,
And here with three Wives he waits till again
The Trumpet shall arouse him to sing out *Amen.*

239. On Mr. Combe, by Shakespeare.

Shakespeare, whose epitaph has already been given in this book, in his latter years, whilst residing in his native town of Stratford, was requested by one of his intimate and wealthy friends, named Mr. Combe, to write his epitaph. The immortal bard furnished him with the following impromptu:—

Ten in the hundred* lies here engraved;
'Tis a hundred to ten his soul is not saved;

---

* Ten per cent. was then the ordinary interest of money.

If any man ask who lies in this tomb,
"O—ho!" quoth the *devil*, "'Tis my John-a-Combe."

240. By Ben Jonson, on ELIZABETH L. H. :—

   Would'st thou hear what man say
   In a little? reader, stay:
   Underneath this stone doth lie
   As much beauty as could die;
   Which in life did harbour give
   To more virtue than doth live.
   If at all she had a fault,
   Leave it buried in this vault.
   One name was ELIZABETH,
   The other, let it sleep with death;
   Fitter, where it died, to tell,
   Than that it lived at all.   Farewell.

241. On a Tailor's Wife.

A tailor, whose Christian name was Abraham, met with the Earl of Rochester, and desired him to write an epitaph for his wife, whose name was SARAH. The Earl complied, and wrote one in his usual ludicrous style, which ran as follows :—

> From Abraham's bosom full of lice,
> To Abraham's in Paradise,
> Our sister SARAH took her flight,
> And bid the lousy thief good-night.

The following is another epitaphian effusion of his:—

242. On KING CHARLES:—

> Here lies our mutton-eating King,
>   Whose word no man relies on;
> He never said a foolish thing,
>   And never did a wise one.

243. On NICHOLAS FERRY, a French Dwarf.

He died at the age of twenty-three, and measured thirty-three inches in height; was, whilst alive, under the protection of the Duke of Lorraine. It is said that the Duke felt his loss severely, and caused an epitaph in Latin to be inscribed on his tomb, of which the following is a translation:—

Here lies
NICHOLAS FERRY,
A Lorraine.
Nature's plaything. In virtue of the smallness of his
Stature he was beloved by the modern
Antoninus,
Old in the flower of existence. For him five lustres
were an age.
He died on the 9th of June, in the year 1764.

(See No. 249 for an epitaph on another dwarf.)

244. On a Woman :—

Underneath this sod lies ARABELLA YOUNG,
Who on the 5th of May began to hold her tongue.

245. From a Churchyard in Yorkshire :—

In faith she dies,
Within she lies,
Here underneath,
Though without breath.

246. From Henley, 1799 :—

A loving Husband, tender Father, and sincere friend,
A generous and an honest man unto his end ;

Always inclin'd to serve his friends when in trouble
Doubtless, by the Lord he'll be rewarded double.

247. From Banbury Churchyard, Oxon:—

To the memory of RIC. RICHARDS, who by gangreen first lost a toe, afterwards a leg, and lastly his life, on the 7th day of April, 1656 :—

Ah, cruel Death, to make three meals of one,
To taste and eat, and eat till all was gone;
But, know, thou tyrant, when the trump shall call,
He'll find his feet, and stand when thou shalt fall.

248. On the REV. JOHN CHEST :—

Beneath this spot lies buried
One CHEST within another,
The outer chest was a good one :
Who says so of the other?

249. On a Dwarf.

The following inscription—on a dwarf who was very intellectual and had great skill on the piano —to be found on a tombstone in the graveyard of St. Philip's in Birmingham, expresses the opinion which was entertained of her by all who knew her:—

> In memory of MANNETTA STOCKER,
> who quitted this life the fourth day of May,
> 1819, at the age of thirty-nine years.
> The smallest woman in this kingdom, and
> one of the most accomplished.
> She was not more than thirty-three inches high.
> She was a native of Austria.

250. From the Churchyard of Castell-llwchwr, South Wales:—

> O Earth! O Earth, observe this well,
> That Earth to Earth must go to dwell,
> That Earth in Earth must close remain
> Till Earth for Earth shall come again.

251. From the same Churchyard, now called Loughor:—

The following pretty lines are now visible on the tomb of MARY PENGREE, who died in 1801, aged 10 years:—

> The village maidens to her Grave shall bring
> The fragrant Garland each returning spring;

Selected sweets, in emblem of the maid
Who underneath the hollow turf is laid.
Like her they flourish, beauteous to the eye;
Like her, too soon, they languish, fade, and die.

252. From Yate Churchyard, Gloucestershire :—

Here lies two whom death again has wed,
And made this grave their second marriage bed.
Death did at first raise some disconsolation,
But would not make an utter separation.

253. In Dunmore Churchyard, Ireland :—

Here lie the remains of JOHN HALL, grocer. The world is not worth a *fig*, and I have good *raisins* for saying so.

254. From Chipping Sodbury, Gloucestershire. On SAMUEL TURNER, Blacksmith :—

His sledge and hammer lie reclined,
His bellows, too, has lost its wind,
His Coal is spent, his Iron gone,
His nails are drove, his work is done.
His body's here, clutched in the dust,
'Tis hoped his soul is with the just.

255. On Mr. Horse :—

>A generous foe, a faithful friend,
>A victor bold, here met his end ;
>He conquer'd both in war and peace ;
>By death subdued, his glories cease.
>Ask'st thou who finished here his course,
>With so much honour?—'twas a HORSE.

256. On John Sullen :—

>Here lies JOHN SULLEN, and it is God's will
>He that was Sullen should be Sullen still ;
>He still is Sullen, if the truth ye seek ;
>Knock until doomsday, Sullen will not speak.

257. An Epigrammatic one :—

>>Beneath yon humble clod at rest,
>>Lies ANDREW, who, if not the best,
>>>Was not the very worst man ;
>>A little rakish, apt to roam,
>>But not so now, he's quite at home,
>>>For Andrew was a Dustman.

258. From Rothsay :—

Erected by JANE ———, to the memory of her husband JOHN ———. "Him that cometh unto me I will in no wise cast out."

259. From Chichester Cathedral.

At the north-west corner is a vault belonging to Mr. Gay, in the centre of which is a fine piece of sculpture. On a pedestal is represented *Time*, in a sitting posture, holding an hourglass in his left hand—the right hand extended, holding a scroll, on which are inscribed the following beautiful and expressive lines:—

> Here doubtless many a trifler on the brink
>   Of this world's hazardous and headlong shore,
> Forc'd to a pause, will feel it good to think,
>   Told that his setting sun may rise no more!
> Ye self-deceived: could I prophetic say,
>   Who next is fated, and who next shall fall,
> The rest might then seem privileged to play;
>   But naming none, TIME'S voice here speaks to all!
> Learn, then, ye living! by the mouths be taught
>   Of all these sepulchres, instruction true—
> That soon or late, death also is your lot,
>   And the next opening grave may yawn for you!

At the further end of the vault is Death, engraved on a black marble slab.

260. On WILLIAM COWPER, the poet.

The immortal Cowper was buried in St. Edmund's chapel, East Dereham, county of Norfolk, and over his grave a monument is erected, bearing the following inscription, from the pen of Mr. Hayley:—

In memory of WILLIAM COWPER, Esq., born in Herefordshire, 1731, buried in this church, 1800.

> Ye, who with warmth the public triumph feel,
> Of talents dignified by public zeal,
> Here, to devotion's bard devoutly just,
> Pay your fond tribute due to COWPER'S dust!
> England, exulting in his spotless fame,
> Ranks with her dearest sons his fav'rite name;
> Sense, fancy, wit, suffice not all to raise
> So clear a title to affection's praise;
> His highest honours to the heart belong,
> His virtues form the magic of his song.

261. On MR. EDWARD EVERARD, in Tottenham Churchyard:—

> You *was* too good to live on earth with me,
> And I not good enough to die with thee;

Farewell, dear husband, God would have it so;
You'll *near* return, but I to you must go.

262. On the eminent barrister, SIR JOHN STRANGE :—

> Here lies an honest lawyer,—
> that is STRANGE.

263. From Prittlewell Churchyard, near Southend. On THOMAS HALLIDAY, aged 23 :—

How lov'd, how valued once, avails thee not,
To whom related, or by whom begot;
A heap of dust alone remains of me,
'Tis all thou art, and all the proud shall be.

264. From Blackmoor :—

> 26 years I lived single,
> 5 a married life,
> Long time I was afflicted,
> And then I lost my life.

A similarly-worded epitaph is to be seen in Newport Cemetery, in which the writer has had many a quiet and pleasant half-hour; it is as follows :—

265. On SARAH, wife of Rowland Thomas :—

> 34 years i was a maid,
> 9 months 6 days a wedded wife,
> two hours i was a mother,
> and then i lost my life.

266. From Bidstone Churchyard.

Again, there is a very similar epitaph to be found in Bidstone Churchyard, where there is a small sandstone obelisk erected to the memory of a young woman named Martha Clark, *née* Owen. After giving the name and age, the epitaph concludes :—

> Nineteen years a maid,
> Two years a wife,
> Nine days a mother,
> And then departed life.

267. On LORD BYRON.

The following epitaphian inscription is on Lord Byron's monument, which is an elegant Grecian tablet of white marble, placed in the chancel of Hucknal church. The words are in Roman capitals, and divided into lines as under:—

> In the vault beneath,
> where many of his ancestors and his
> mother are buried,
> lie the remains of
> GEORGE GORDON NOEL BYRON,
> Lord Byron of Rochdale,
> in the county of Lancaster:
> The author of " Childe Harold's Pilgrimage."
> He was born in London, on the
> 22nd of January, 1788;
> He died at Missolonghi, in Western
> Greece, on the
> 19th April, 1824,
> Engaged in the glorious attempt to
> restore that country to her ancient
> freedom and renown.
> His sister, the Honourable
> Augusta Maria Leigh,
> placed this tablet to his memory.

268. From East Grinstead, Sussex.

The following is copied from a stone in the churchyard of East Grinstead, in Sussex:—

In memory of RUSSELL HALL
And MARY his wife.
He died March 25, 1816,
Aged 79 years.
She died August 22, 1809,
Aged 58 years.
The ritual stone thy children lay
O'er thy respected dust,
Only proclaims the mournful day
When we our parents lost.
To copy thee in life we'll strive,
And when we that resign
May some good-natured friend survive
To lay our bones by thine.

269. On VIRGIL.

As we have elsewhere given the epitaphs on several poets, we think the following may not prove uninteresting to our readers; it is upon the tomb of VIRGIL, the prince of Roman poets, and is said to have been dictated by himself:—

Mantua me genuit Calabri rapuere tenet nunc Parthenope; cecini Pascua Rura, Duces.

The tomb is situated near Naples.

270. From Peterchurch :—

> Sickness was my portion,
>   Physic was my food,
> Groans was my devotion,
>   Drugs did me no good.
> The Lord took pity on me,
>   Because He thought it best—
> He took me to his bosom,
>   And here I lies at rest.

271. From Michaelchurch :—

JOHN PROSSER is my name, and England is my nation,
Bowchurch is my dwelling-place, and Christ is my salvation ;
Now I'm dead and in my grave, and all my bones are rotten :
As you pass by remember me, when I am quite forgotten.

271*a*. From Hatfield Churchyard, Herts :—

> The world's a city full of crooked streets ;
> And death the *market-place* where all men meet ;
> If death were merchandise, then men could buy :
> The rich would always live, the poor must die.

272. From Dartford Churchyard, Kent :—

We all must die, we know full well,
But when or where no one can tell;
Strive, therefore, to live godly still,
Then welcome death, come when it will.

A PEDESTRIAN.

273. From St. John's Churchyard, Horsleydown. On Captain ——, who was drowned at Gravesend:—

> Friends, cease to grieve that at Gravesend
>   My life was closed with speed,
> For when the Saviour shall descend,
>   'Twill be *graves' end* indeed.

274. From a small and solitary churchyard in Kent:—

Here lyeth the bones of MARY ROGERS, who left this world A.D. 1692; she was a goode mother, wifee, and daughter:

> Al goud people, as you pass,
> Pray *reed* my hour-glass;
> After sweets and bitters it's down,
> And I have left your pretty town.
> Remember soon you must prepare to fly,
> From all your friends, and come to *high*.

275. From the same place:—

This ston his sacred to the memory of poer old Muster THOMAS BOXER, who was loste in the goud boate Rouver, just coming home with much fishes, got near Torbay, in the year of hour Lord 1722:

>Prey, goud fishermen, stop and drop a tear,
>For we have lost his company here;
>And where he's gone we cannot tell;
>But we hope far from the wicked Bell.
>   The Lord be with him.

276. From the same place:—

To the memory of my four wives, who all died within the space of ten years, but more *pertickler* to the last, MRS. SALLY HORNE, who has left me and four dear children: she was a good, *sober*, and *clean soul*, and may i soon go to her—A.D. 1732:

>Dear wives, if you and i shall all go to heaven,
>The Lord be blest, for then we shall be even,
>   WILLIAM JOY HORNE, Carpenter.

277. From Barking, Essex. On SARAH RICKETTS, aged 68, 1767:—

> Here honest SARAH RICKETTS lies,
> By many much esteem'd,
> Who really was no otherwise
> Than what she ever seemed.

278. From Lee, Essex. On MR. WILLIAM HAMPTON :—

> As *Mary* mourn'd to find the stone removed
> From o'er the Lord, who was her best belov'd,
> So *Mary* mourns that here hath laid this stone
> Upon the best belovèd husband gone.

279. On JOHN COLE, who died suddenly while at dinner :—

> Here lies JOHNNY COLE,
> Who died, on my soul,
> After eating a plentiful dinner;
> While chewing his crust,
> He was turn'd into dust,
> With his crimes *undigested*, poor sinner!

280. From Leigh Delamere Churchyard, Wilts:—

> Who lies here? Who do 'e think?
> Why, old CLAPPER WATTS, if you'll give him some
> Give a dead man drink?—for why?   [drink.
> Why, when he was alive he was always a-dry.

281. From Lambeth Churchyard, on WILLIAM WILSON :—

> Here lieth W. W.
> Who never more will trouble you, trouble you.

282. On a Miser :—

Reader, beware of immoderate love of pelf:
Here lies the worst of thieves, who robbed himself.

283. From the Old Cemetery, Newport, Monmouthshire :—

On JAMES AUSTIN, Engine-driver.

> "He was a man."
> SHAKESPEARE.

284. From the same place. On a Scotch Piper:—

To the memory of MR. JOHN MACBETH, late piper to His Grace the Duke of Sutherland, and a native of the Highlands of Scotland:

> Died April 24th, 1852, Aged 46 years.
> Far from his native land, beneath this stone,
> Lies JOHN MACBETH, in prime of manhood gone;
> A kinder husband never yet did breathe,
> A finer friend ne'er trod on Albyn's heath;
> His selfish aims were all in heart and hand,

To be an honour to his native land,
As real Scotchmen wish to fall or stand;
A handsome *Gael* he was of splendid form,
Fit for a siege, or for the Northern Storm.
Sir Walter Scott remarked at Inverness,
"How well becomes Macbeth the Highland dress!"
His mind was stored with ancient Highland lore;
Knew Ossian's songs, and many Bards of yore;
But music was his chief, and soul's delight,
And oft he played, with Amphion's skill and might,
His Highland pipe, before our Gracious Queen!
'Mong Ladies gay and Princesses serene!
His magic chanter's strains pour'd o'er their hearts,
With thrilling rapture soft as Cupid's darts!
Like Shakespeare's witches, scarce they drew the breath
But wished like them to say, "All hail, Macbeth!"
The Queen, well pleased, gave him, by high command,
A splendid present from her Royal hand!
But nothing aye could make him vain or proud,
He felt alike at Court, or in a crowd;
With high and low his nature was to please,
Frank with the Peasant, with the Prince at ease.
Beloved by thousands till his race was run,
Macbeth had ne'er a foe beneath the sun;
And now he plays among the Heavenly bands,
A diamond chanter never made with hands.

285. From Wosborough Churchyard :—

> Here lyeth the body of ISABELLA, the wife of John
> CARRINGTON :
> Who had 9 children deare,
> 4 died before her,
> 5 are living heare;
> Kind to her husband,
> Faithful to her friend,
> And a loving mother,
> Till her life did end.
> Who departed this life 6th Aug., 1674.

286. From Wortley Churchyard :—

> WILLIAM ROGERS, of Bank, died August 29th, 1771,
> aged 49.
> The man that lies here
> To pride was not inclined;
> By endeavours and care
> He left something behind.

287. From the Wesleyan Chapel, Wakefield :—

> Her manners mild, her temper such!
> Her language good, and not too much.

288. From America.

The following is the conclusion of an epitaph on a tombstone in East Tenessee :—

"She lived a life of virtue, and died of cholera morbus, caused by eating green fruit, in the full hope of a blessed immortality, at the early age of twenty-one years, seven months, and sixteen days. Reader, go thou and do likewise."

289. On the Distinguished Clown, GRIMALDI :—
Here I am.

290. On the Comedian, Foote :—

FOOTE from his earthly stage, alas! is hurled :
Death took him off who took off all the world.

291. On the Actress, MRS. OLDFIELD :—

This we must own in justice to her shade,
'Tis the first bad exit OLDFIELD ever made.

292. From Clerkenwell Churchyard :—

Near this monitor of human instability are deposited the remains of ANN, the wife of ———. She resigned her life the 8th day of November, 1784, aged thirty-seven years.

> She was!—
> But words are wanting to say what!
> Think what a wife *should* be,
> And she was that.

(See Nos. 4, 189, and 196.)

293. From Caermarthen Churchyard :—

> The Old must go, Wee all agree,
> So must the Young, Wee plainly see.
> Repent in time, and seek for Grace,
> This world is no abiding place.

294. From the same place :—

> Praises on tombs are trifles vainly spent,
> A man's good name is his best monument.

295. From the same place. On THOMAS HUGHES, Mariner :—

> Having served for many
> Years in the royal navy,
> He spent his later years
> In the costing trade.

296. From the same place, on the tomb of THOS. JONES, ESQ. :—

This notice is here given, if any person or Persons do any Damage to this Tombstone will be subject to a Penalty of Hundred Pounds for such deed, to be paid to the official Clergyman of this Parish.

297. From Wrexham Churchyard :—

> Born in America, in Europe bred,
> In Africa travell'd, and in Asia wed.

298. From Byford Churchyard :—

> As you are in health, and spirits gay,
> I was, too, the other day;
> I thought myself of life as safe
> As those that read my epitaph.

299. From Wrexham Churchyard :—

> Here lies five babes and children dear,
> Three at Oswestry, and two here.

(See No. 176.)

300. From the same place :—

> Here lies Jane Shore,
> I say no more,
> Who was alive—
> In sixty-five.

301. From New Jersey:—

> Died of thin shoes, January, 1839.

302. On CRETHON of Tarentum:—

> Who once had wealth, not less than Gyges' gold;
> Who once was rich in stable, stall, and fold;
> Who once was blessed above all other men
> With lands—how narrow now, so ample then.

The idea here contained is nicely amplified i Shakespeare's play of *Henry IV.*, Act v., Scene ¿ Prince Henry, as he bends over the falle Hotspur, says:—

> When that his body did contain a spirit,
> A kingdom for it was too small a bound;
> But now two paces of the vilest earth is room enoug

303. From Tamworth Churchyard:—

> . To the memory of
> MARY KNIGHT, aged 25:

She faded from the sight as flowers
In summer fade; she vanished as the rain
After sultry showers; she sank pale and lovely,
Like the fleecy snow, which in the sunbeam
Melts; and we have laid her in her peaceful
Resting-place, to wait the coming of her Lord.

304. From Painswick Churchyard, near Stroud, Gloucestershire :—

> My wife is dead, and here she lies,
> Nobody laughs and nobody cries;
> Where she is gone to, or how she fares,
> Nobody knows, and nobody cares.

305. From Ireland :—

> Here lies MRS. CASEYS,
> Who taking her *aise* is,
>   With the points of her toes
>   And the tip of her nose
> Turned up to the roots of the daisies.

306. From Wales :—

> She had two bad legs and a very bad cough,
> But it was the bad legs that *carried* her off.

This is on the authority of Major Austin, bu[t]
I am informed a fuller edition of it is to be see[n]
in a Devonshire Churchyard. (See 310.)

307. From a Churchyard near London :—

> Stop, reader! I have left a world
> In which there was a world to do;
> Fretting and stewing to be rich—
> Just such a fool as you.

308. From St. Mary's, Shrewsbury :—

> Let this small monument record the name
> Of BADMAN, and to future times proclaim
> How, by 'n attempt to fly from this high spire,
> Across the Sabrine stream, he did acquire
> His fatal end. 'Twas not for want of skill,
> Or courage to perform the task, he fell;
> No, no; a faulty cord being drawn too tight,
> Hurried his soul on high to take her flight,
> Which bid the body here good-night.
>   Feb. 2nd, 1739. Aged 28.

309. From Wapley, Gloucestershire :—

> A time of death there is,
> you know full well.

But when, or how 'twill come,
   no man can tell.
At midnight, morn, or noon:
   remember then,
Death is most certain, though
   uncertain when.

310. From Devonshire :—

Poor MARY SNELL, her's gone away;
Her would if her could,
   But her couldn't stay;
Her had sore legs, and a baddish cough,
But her legs it were that carried her off.

311. From Lichfield, Connecticut:—

Sacred to the memory of inestimable worth, of unrivalled excellence and virtue [then the name], whose ethereal parts became seraphic on the 25th day of May, 1867.

312. From San Diego :—

Here lies the body of JAMES HAMBRICK, who was accidentally shot on the Pacus River by a young man. He was accidentally shot with one of the large Colt's revolvers, with no stopper for the cock to rest on. It was one of the old-fashioned kind, brass-mounted, and of such is the kingdom of Heaven.

313. On a Linen-draper:—

> Cotton and calicos all adieu,
>   And muslins, too, farewell;
> Plain, striped, and figured, old and new,
>   Three-quarter, yard, or ell.
> By nail and yard I've measured ye,
>   As customers inclined.
> The churchyard now has measured me,
>   And nails my coffin bind.

314. From Llanfylantwthyl, Wales. On an Organ Blower:—

> Under this stone lies MEREDITH MORGAN,
> Who blew the bellows of our church organ.
> Tobacco he hated, to smoke most unwilling,
> Yet never so pleased as when *pipes* he was filling.
> No reflection on him for rude speech could be cast,
> Though he gave our old organ many a blast!
> No puffer was he, though a capital blower;
> He could blow double C, and now lies a note lower.

315. From Bury St. Edmunds. On a Printer:—

Like a worn-out type he is returned to the founder, in hopes of being re-cast in a better and more perfect mould.

316. From a Churchyard in Essex :—

>Here lies the man RICHARD,
>　And MARY his wife;
>Their surname was PRITCHARD,
>　They lived without strife.
>And the reason was plain :
>　They abounded in riches,
>They had no care or pain,
>　And the wife wore the breeches.

317. On MR. JONES, a celebrated bone merchant :—

>Here lies the bones of WILLIAM JONES,
>Who, when alive, collected bones ;
>But Death, that bony, grizzly spectre,
>That most amazing bone collector,
>Has boned poor Jones so snug and tidy,
>That here he lies in *bonâ fide*.

318. On a Photographer :—

>Here I am, *taken from life.*

319. On a Mrs. PENNY :—

> Reader, if cash thou art in want of any,
> Dig five-feet deep, and you will find a PENNY.

320. From Penclawdd Churchyard, near Swansea Upon an only child :—

I will make my first-born higher than the Kings of the Earth.

321. From Mathern Churchyard, Chepstow :—

To the memory of JOSEPH LEE, who died in 1825, aged 103 years.

> Joseph Lee is dead and gone,
> We ne'er shall see him more;
> He used to wear an old drab coat,
> All buttoned down before.

322. On "JOHNNIE LADDIE."

In the Brachlach burying-place, near the Fort George Station, may be seen the following epitaph on one of the tombstones there :—

Sacred to the memory of a character, JOHN CAMERON, "Johnnie Laddie," a native of Campbeltown, Ardersier, who died there August 26, 1858, aged 65 years. Erected to his memory by public subscription :

> Sixty winters on the street,
> No shoes nor stockings on his feet ;
> Amusement both to small and great,
> Was poor " Johnnie Laddie."

323. From Poundstick Churchyard, Cornwall :—

> Both soul and body coming here to try
> The things of earth they found but vanity ;]
> So shaking hands with all he left in love,
> His body's here, his better part's above.

324. From Bakewell, Derbyshire :—

> The local powers here let us mark
> Of PHILIP, our late Parish clerk :
> In church none ever heard a layman,
> With a clearer voice say Amen.
> Who now with Hallelujah's sound
> Like him can make the roof rebound ?
> The choirs lament his choral tones,
> The town so soon—here lie his bones.

325. From the same place :—

> In memory of JOHN DALE.

Know, all posterity, that in the year of grace 1797 the rambling remains of the above said John Dale were laid upon his two wives:

> This thing in life might cause some jealousy:
> Here all three lay together lovingly;
> But from embraces here no pleasure flows,
> Alike are here all human joys and woes.
> Here old JOHN'S rambling SARAH no more fears.
> And Sarah's chiding John no longer hears;
> A period's come to all their toilsome lives:
> The good man's quiet. Still are both his wives.

326. From Leek Churchyard :—

> As I was, so be ye;
> As I am, ye shall be;
> That I gave, that I have;
> What I spent, that I had;
> Thus I end all my cost;
> What I left, that I lost.

327. From Montmarte Cemetery :—

> Here lies A. B.
> Who at the age of eighteen
> earned £40 a year.

328. From a tombstone in Connecticut:—

> Here lies, cut down like unripe fruit,
> The wife of Deacon AMOS SHUTE:
> She died of drinking too much coffee,
> Anny Dominy eighteen forty.

329. From Bolton Churchyard, Lancashire:—

> She was, but words fail me to say what—
> Just think what a wife should be, and she was that.

(See Nos. 4, 189, 196, and 292.)

330. From Bath Abbey:—

> Here lies ANN MANN;
> She lived an old *Maid* and she died an old *Mann*.

The pun of the above is equalled by the epitaph

331. On OWEN MOORE:—

> OWEN MOORE is gone away,
> Owin' more than he could pay.

332. From Wrexham Church:—

> Here lies interr'd beneath these stones
> The beard, the flesh, and eke ye bones
> Of Wrexham's clerk, old DANIEL JONES.

333. From Silkstone Churchyard :—

JOHN TAYLOR, of Silkston, potter, died July 14th, 1815, aged 72; HANNAH his wife, died August 13th, 1815, aged 68 :

> Out of the clay they got their bread;
> Themselves of clay (or dust) were made;
> To clay returned, they now lie dead;
> In churchyard clay all must be laid.
> His wife to live without him tried,
> Hard found the task, fell sick and died;
> And now in peace their bodies lie,
> Until the dead be called on high,
> New moulded for their home—the sky.

334. From Edinburgh :—

> Here lies JOHN and his Wife
> JANET MCFEE:
> 40 hee—30 shee.

335. On THOMAS DAY :—

> Here lies TOMMY DAY,
> Removed from over the way.

336. From Lambeth Churchyard, Surrey:—

> On MARY, the wife of WILLIAM CUBETT, who died February 2nd, 1785, aged 51.
> She was, but words are wanting to say what—
> Think what a wife should be, and she was that.

(See Nos. 4, 189, 196, 292, and 329.)

337. On MR. WOODCOCK :—

> Here lies the body of Thomas WOODHEN,
> The most loving of husbands and amiable of men.
>
> N.B.—His name was *Woodcock*, but it wouldn't rhyme.
>
> Erected by his loving widow.

338. On a Barren Woman :—

> Here lies the body of barren PEG,
> Who had no issue but one in her leg;
> But while she was living she was so cunning
> That when one stood still the other was running.

339. On Sir WILLIAM CURTIS :—

> Here lies WILLIAM CURTIS, late our Lord Mayor,
> Who has left this here world and gone to that there.

340. On a Coroner who hanged himself:—

> He lived and died
> By suicide.

341. From St. Nicholas, Yarmouth :—

> Here lyeth yᵉ body of
> SARAH BLOOMFIELD,
> Aged 74.
> Cut off in blooming yuthe, we can but pity.

342. From Pewsey Churchyard :—

> Here lies the body of
> LADY O'LOONEY,
> Great niece of Burke, commonly called
> the sublime ;
> She was
> Bland, passionate, and deeply religious :
> Also she painted in water-colours,
> And sent several pictures to the Exhibition.
> She was first cousin to Lady Jones.
> And of such is the kingdom of heaven.

343. On a Quack :—

> I was a Quack, and there are men who say
> That in my time I physicked men away,

And that at length I by myself was slain,
By my own doings ta'en to relieve my pain.
The truth is, being troubled with a cough,
I, like a fool, consulted Dr. Gough,
Who physicked to death at his own will,
Because he's licensed by the State to kill.
Had I but wisely taken my own physic
I never should have died of cold and 'tisick.
So all be warned, and when you catch a cold
Go to my son, by whom my medicine's sold.

344. On a Teetotaller. Taken from the *European Magazine* of March, 1796:—

Here lies NED RAND, who on a sudden,
Left off roast beef for hasty pudding;
Forsook old stingo, mild, and stale,
And every drink for Adam's ale;
Till flesh and blood, reduced to batter,
Consisting of mere flour and water,
Which, wanting salt to keep out must,
And heat to bake it to a crust,
Mouldered and crumbled into dust.

345. From Dortmund Cemetery, Westphalia:—

Heinrich Bruggeman heissich,
Nach dem Himmel reise ich,

>   Will mal seh'n was Jesus macht,
>   Liebe Bruder, gute nacht.

346. On ROBIN HOOD:—

>   Hear underneath this latil stean
>   Laiz ROBERT EARL of Huntington,
>   Nea arcir ver az hie sa geud,
>   An pipel kauld him Robin Heud.
>   Sich atlaz az he an iz men
>   Vil England nior si agen.
>   Obit 24 Kalend, Dikimbris, 1247.

347. From Hewelsfield, near St. Briavels:—

>   Farewell, vain World, I know enough of thee,
>   I value not what thou canst say of me;
>   Thy smiles I court not, nor thy frowns I fear;
>   All's one to me, my head lies quiet here:
>   What thou see'st amiss in me take care to shun;
>   Look well at home, there's something to be done.
>   JONNA EDWARDS,
>   of Harthill Court,
>   Died November 14th, 1838.

348. From St. Nicholas', Yarmouth:—

>   Here lies JOHN MOORE, a miser old,
>   Who filled his cellar with Silver and Gold.

(h) Old Moore he cried, old Moore, old Moore,
'Twas clear he would not close the door,
And yet cried (h) Old Moore, Old Moore.

349. From the same place, on a Dyer :—

> Here lies a man who first did dye
>   When he was 24,
> And yet he lived to reach the age
>   Of hoary hairs fourscore.
> But now he's gone, and certain 'tis
>   He'll not dye any more

350. From the same place :—

> Here lies JOHN WHEEDLE, Parish Beedle,
>   Who was so very knowing;
> His wisdom's gone, and so is he,
>   Because he left off growing.

351. From the same place :—

> Here lies one, a sailor's bride,
> Who widowed was because of the tide;
> It drowned her husband—so she died.

352. On a Member of the House of Lords :—

Ultimum Domum:

Did he who wrote upon this wall,
Ere read or disbelieve ST. PAUL?
Who tells us that in foreign lands
There is a house not made with hands:
Or must we gather from these words
That house is not a House of Lords!

353. From New Jersey :—

She was not smart, she was not fair,
  But hearts with grief for her are swellin';
All empty stands her little chair:
  She died of eatin' water-melon.

354. From Berkeley Churchyard. On a fo[ol]

Here lies the Earl of Suffolk's fool,
  Men called him DICKY PEARCE:
His folly served to make folks laugh,
  When wit and mirth were scarce.
Poor Dick, alas! is dead and gone—
  What signifies to cry!
Dickys enough are still behind,
  To laugh at by-and-by.

355. From the same place :—

Here lyeth THOMAS PEIRCE, whom no man taught,
Yet he in Iron, Brasse, and silver wrought;
He Jacks, and Clocks, and watches (with Art) made
And mended, too, when other worke did fade.
Of Berkeley five tymes Mayor this Artist was,
And yet this Mayor, this Artist, was but Grasse.
When his own Watch was Downe on the last Day,
He that made watches had not made a Key,
To wind it Vp, but Vselesse it must lie,
Until he Rise AGaine no more to die!
    Deceased the 25th of February, 1665, Ætatis, 77.

356. On a Pig-butcher at Cheltenham :—

>   Here lies a true and honest man,
>   You scarce would find such a one in ten;
>   For killing pigs was his delight,
>   Which art he practised day and night.

357. From Hewelsfield, near St Briavels. On HENRY BROWN, who died Sept. 10, 1794, aged 48 years :

>   It was an Imposthume
>   in my Breast

> That brought me to
> eternal Rest.

358. On a Good Wife. From Streatham Church, Surrey :—

> REBECCA, wife of WILLIAM LYNNE,
> who died in 1663.

> Might I ten thousand years enjoy my life,
> I could not praise enough so good a wife.

359. A monument in the same church bears testimony to the virtues of

> ELIZABETH, wife of Major-Gen. Hamilton,
> who was married near forty-seven years,
> and
> Never did one thing to disoblige her husband.
> She died in 1746.

360. From the Churchyard of Aloes, Elgin, the following account of another Good Wife is copied from a gravestone dated 1580 :—

EPITAPHIANA.

Here lies
ANDERSON OF PITTENSEN,
Maire of the Earldom of Moray,
With his wife Marjory,
Whilk him never displicit.

361. On an Author :—

FINIS.

INDEX TO NOTED AND EMINENT CHARACTERS.

NOTE.—The Figures refer to the Number of the Epitaph.

ANGLER, on an	197
Anonymous	230
Author, on an	361
BANCROFT, Archbishop	62
Barren Woman	338
Barras, Robert	184
Baskerville, John	73
Beck, William	188
Bennett, James Gordon	102
Bentley, Dr.	126
Blundering epitaphs	110, 111, 112
Bone Merchant, on a	317
Boxer, on a	71
Briefest on record	161
Brothers, on two	186
Brougham, Lord	39
Bunn, John	141
Burns, Robert	67
Byron, Lord	267
CARDINAL, on a	116
Charles, King	242
Chantres, Col.	236
Chest, Rev. John	248
Child, on a	140
Cole, John	279
Collier, on a	179
Collier, John	44
Combe, Mr.	239
Copernicus	104
Corbett, Mr.	205
Coroner, on a	340
Country Sexton, on a	10, 69
Cowper, William	260
Crethon	302
Curtis, Sir William	339
DAY, THOMAS	335
Draper, on a	313
Dryden, Mrs.	172
Dwarf, on a	249
ELIZABETH L. H.	240
Ennui, on one troubled with	199
Epigrammatic	157, 257
FERGUSSON, ROBERT	83
Fiddler, on a	192
Foote the Comedian	290
Franklin, Dr.	106
French Dwarf	243
Freeland, Rebecca	173
Friday, unlucky Ship	212
GOLD-DIGGER, on a	159
Greenwood, Dr., Wife of	72
Grimaldi the Clown	289
Grindstone, from a	25
Grose, Francis	50
HILL, JOHN	154
Hogarth	150
Hood, Robin	346
Horse, Mr.	255
Husband and wife	181

INDEX.

Icy One, an 149
Infant, on an . . . 120, 146
Infidel, on an 24
Italian, on an 21

James, G. P. R. . . . 118
Jack and Joan . . . 237
"Jerusalem Delivered," on the
  Author of . . . 162
Joblin, George . . . 19
Jonson, Ben . . . 80, 163

Kemp, Thomas . . 210a
Killed by a pump . . . 232
Knight, Charles . . . 86

Laddie, Johnnie . . . 322
Landlord, on a . . . 74
Lawyer, on a 16
Llewellyn, William . . 91
London Cook . . . 32
Long, Miss 64
Lords, Member of House of . 352

McPherson John . . 142
Miser, on a 202
Miser, on a . 2, 29, 31, 66, 282
Moore, Owen 331
Mum, Susan 187
Musician, on a . . . 207

Newton, Sir Isaac . . 203
Ned, Honest 55
Norton, Roger . . . 148
N., E. 23

Oldfield, Mrs., the Actress. 291
Old one 139
Organ Blower, on an . . 314

Painter, on a . . . 225
Pardon, Edward . . . 200
Parnell, Thomas . . . 82
Penny, Mrs. 319
Phonetic epitaph . . . 109
Photographer, on a . . 318
Poet, on a 42
Pope Adrian 204

Popish epitaph . . . 99
Political one 103
Potter, Dr. 170
Prior, Matthew . . . 210
Provost of Dundee . . . 13

Quack, on a 343
Queer epitaph . . . 158

Rich Man, on a . . 180, 221a
Rosewell, John . . . 166

Sailor, on a 228
Saul, Daniel 58
Scott, Margery . . . 49
Shakespeare 9
Simple one 155
Smoker, on a 208
So, John 12
Spendthrift, on a . . . 77
Steel, Pat 90
Stokes, Mrs. 143
Stone, Mrs. 144
Strange, Sir John . . . 262
Sullen, John 256
Surgeon, on a . . . 43

Tailor's Wife, on a . . 241
Teetotaler, on a . . . 344
Tessin, Count . . . 201
Thumb, Christopher . . 152
Tippler, on a . . . 125

Violinist, on a bad . . 135
Virgil 269

Wesleyan Minister . . 175
White, John 169
Wife, on a 54, 160, 358, 359, 360
Wife, on a French . . . 131
Wife, on a Virtuous . . 127
Woodcock, Mr. . . . 337
Wotton, Sir Henry . . 85
Woman, on a . . . 244
Wren, Sir Christopher . . 174

Yorkshire Cook . . . 89

INDEX TO PLACES.

NOTE.—The Figures refer to the Number of the Epitaph.

Place	Epitaph	Place	Epitaph
ABERCONWAY	137	Cambridge	220
Alban's, St., Abbey	123	Cameley, Somerset	107
Aldersgate	75	Cheltenham	231, 356
Allowa	119	Cherening-le-Clay	94
America	5, 35, 101, 102, 222, 235, 288, 311, 328	Chichester	63, 259
		Chipping Sodbury	254
Anglesey	96	Churchill	92
Arlington	98, 124	Clerkenwell	292
		Clevedon	76
BABINGTON	108	Cork	99
Bakewell	324, 325	Cracow	104
Banbury	247	Crayford	238
Barking	277	Creltow	211
Barrow	168	Crimea	18
Barrow-upon-Soar	97	Curmwallen	178
Barton Stacey	68		
Barton	38	DARTFORD	272
Bath	33, 45, 46, 47, 330	Devizes	87
Belturbet	151	Devonshire	17, 310
Berkeley	354, 355	Dortmund, Westphalia	345
Beverley	121	Dunmore, Ireland	253
Bideford	3		
Bidston	266	EAST GRINSTEAD	268
Birmingham	159	Edinburgh	51, 334
Bishop's Canning	70	Ely	145
Blakemore	264	Essex	316
Bolton	329	Eton College	84
Brancepeth	223	Everton	156
Bride's, St.	233	Eton	15
Bristol	95, 114		
Broom	185	FROME	152
Bruton	229		
Bury St. Edmunds	147, 315	GLOUCESTER	41
Byford	298	Grantham	60
CAERMARTHEN	293, 294, 295, 296	HANWELL	224

INDEX.

Hatfield	271a
Henley	246
Hereford	133
Hewelsfield, near St. Briavels	347, 357
High Wycombe	209
Hordle, near Lymington	44
Horsleydown	78, 273
Houghton, Hunts	20
Hyden	153
IRELAND	34, 305
JERSEY	122
KARL KEEL	111
Kensal Green	215, 217
Kent	274, 275, 276
Kingston	22
LAMBETH	281, 336
Lee	278
Leek	326
Leigh Delamere	280
Llangerrig	7, 8
London	307
Loughor	250, 251
Lydford	28
MAIDSTONE	216
Marnhull	14
Melrose	105
Michaelchurch	271
Monkwearmouth	4
Montgomeryshire	40
Montrose	112
Montmartre	327
Morville	219
NAPLES	270
Nettlebed, Oxfordshire	138
Newbury	130
Newington	129
New Jersey	301, 354
Newport, Mon.	265, 283, 284
New York	164
Northampton	115
Norwich Cathedral	136
OCKHAM	27
Oldbury-on-Severn	183
PAINSWICK	304
Paul's Wharf, London	128
Pembrokeshire	177
Penclawdd	320
Pewsey	342
Plymouth	110
Portsmouth	234
Poundstock	323
Preston, near Weymouth	1
Prittlewell	263
RIPON CATHEDRAL	134
Rome	221
Rothesay	258
Royton	30
SALISBURY	61
San Diego	312
Scotland	81
Selby	227
Shoreditch	193
Shrewsbury	308
Silkstone	333
South Wales	176
St. Paul's	65
Staffordshire	117
Sussex	53
Swaffham	214
Swansea	189, 190, 195, 196, 198, 206
TAIBACH	213
Tamworth	303
Taunton	191
Thornton	113
Torryburn	182
Tottenham	261
UPTON-ON-SEVERN	100
VENICE	132
WAKEFIELD	287
Wales	6, 57, 306, 314
Wapley	309
Webley	226

Wedmore 93	Wrexham . 297, 299, 300, 332
Westminster Abbey . . 171	
Whitby 194	YARMOUTH 341, 348, 349, 350, 351
Winchester 56	Yate 252
Woolstanton 167	York 88
Wortley 286	Yorkshire 245
Wosborough 285	

THE END.

Watson and Hazell, Printers, London and Aylesbury.

NOVEMBER, 1875.

SAMUEL TINSLEY'S

PUBLICATIONS.

London:
SAMUEL TINSLEY,
10, SOUTHAMPTON STREET, STRAND.

✱ *Totally distinct from any other firm of Publishers.*

NOTICE.

The PRINTING and PUBLICATION of all Classes of BOOKS, Pamphlets, &c.— Apply to MR. SAMUEL TINSLEY, *Publisher, 10, Southampton Street, Strand, London, W.C.*

SAMUEL TINSLEY'S
NEW PUBLICATIONS.

THE POPULAR NEW NOVELS, AT ALL LIBRARIES IN TOWN AND COUNTRY.

A DESPERATE CHARACTER: a Tale of the Gold Fever. By W. THOMSON-GREGG. 3 vols., 31s. 6d.
"A novel which cannot fail to interest."—*Daily News.*

ALDEN OF ALDENHOLME. By GEORGE SMITH. 3 vols., 31s. 6d.

ALICE GODOLPHIN and A LITTLE HEIRESS. By MARY NEVILLE. In 2 vols. 21s.

A NAME'S WORTH. By Mrs. M. ALLEN. 2 vols., 21s.

A WIDOW OF WINDSOR. By ANNIE GASKELL. Crown 8vo, 7s. 6d.

ANNALS of the TWENTY-NINTH CENTURY; or, the Autobiography of the Tenth President of the World-Republic. 3 vols., 31s. 6d.

"From beginning to end the book is one long catalogue of wonders.... Very amusing, and will doubtless create some little sensation."—*Scotsman.*

"Here is a work in certain respects one of the most singular in modern literature, which surpasses all of its class in bold and luxuriant imagination, in vivid descriptive power, in startling—not to say extravagant suggestions —in lofty and delicate moral sympathies. It is difficult to read it with a serious countenance: yet it is impossible not to read it with curious interest, and sometimes with profound admiration. The author's imagination hath run mad, but often there is more in his philosophy than the world may dream of..... We have read his work with almost equal feelings of pleasure, wonderment, and amusement, and this, we think, will be the feelings of most of its readers. On the whole, it is a book of remarkable novelty and unquestionable genius."—*Nonconformist.*

A SACRIFICE TO HONOUR. By Mrs. HENRY LYTTELTON ROGERS. Crown 8vo, 7s. 6d.

AS THE FATES WOULD HAVE IT. By G. BERESFORD FITZGERALD. Crown 8vo., 10s. 6d.

Samuel Tinsley, 10, Southampton Street, Strand.

A WOMAN TO BE WON. An Anglo-Indian Sketch. By ATHENE BRAMA. 2 vols., 21s.

"She is a woman, therefore may be wooed ;
She is a woman, therefore may be won."
—TITUS ANDRONICUS, Act ii., Sc. 1.

"A welcome addition to the literature connected with the most picturesque of our dependencies."—*Athenæum.*

"As a tale of adventure 'A Woman to be Won' is entitled to decided commendation."—*Graphic.*

"A more familiar sketch of station life in India . . . . has never been written. . . . ."—*Nonconformist.*

BARBARA'S WARNING. By the Author of "Recommended to Mercy." 3 vols., 31s. 6d.

BETWEEN TWO LOVES. By ROBERT J. GRIFFITHS, LL.D. 3 vols., 31s. 6d.

BLUEBELL. By Mrs. G. C. HUDDLESTON. 3 vols., 31s. 6d.

"Sparkling, well-written, spirited, and may be read with certainty of amusement."—*Sunday Times.*

BORN TO BE A LADY. By KATHERINE HENDERSON. Crown 8vo, 7s. 6d.

"Miss Henderson has written a really interesting story. . . . The 'local colouring' is excellent, and the subordinate characters, Jeanie's father especially, capital studies."—*Athenæum.*

BRANDON TOWER. A Story. 3 vols., 31s. 6d.

"Familiar matter of to-day."

BUILDING UPON SAND. By ELIZABETH J. LYSAGHT. Crown 8vo., 10s. 6d.

"We can safely recommend 'Building upon Sand.'"—*Graphic.*

CHASTE AS ICE, PURE AS SNOW. By Mrs. M. C. DESPARD. 3 vols., 31s. 6d. Second Edition.

"A novel of something more than ordinary promise."—*Graphic.*

CINDERELLA : a New Version of an Old Story. Crown 8vo, 7s. 6d.

CLAUDE HAMBRO. By JOHN C. WESTWOOD. 3 vols., 31s. 6d.

CRUEL CONSTANCY. By KATHARINE KING, Author of 'The Queen of the Regiment.' 3 vols., 31s. 6d.

Samuel Tinsley, 10, Southampton Street, Strand.

Samuel Tinsley's Publications.

DISINTERRED. From the Boke of a Monk of Carden Abbey. By T. ESMONDE. Crown 8vo., 7s. 6d.

DR. MIDDLETON'S DAUGHTER. By the Author of "A Desperate Character." 3 vols., 31s. 6d.

DULCIE. By LOIS LUDLOW. 3 vols:, 31s. 6d.

EMERGING FROM THE CHRYSALIS. By J. F. NICHOLLS. Crown 8vo, 7s. 6d.

FAIR, BUT NOT FALSE. By EVELYN CAMPBELL. 3 vols., 31s. 6d.

FAIR, BUT NOT WISE. By Mrs. FORREST-GRANT. 2 vols., 21s.

FIRST AND LAST. By F. VERNON-WHITE. 2 vols., 21s.

FLORENCE; or, Loyal Quand Même. By FRANCES ARMSTRONG. Crown 8vo., 5s., cloth. Post free.

"A very charming love story, eminently pure and lady-like in tone." — *Civil Service Review.*

FAIR IN THE FEARLESS OLD FASHION. By CHARLES FARMLET. 2 vols., 21s.

FOLLATON PRIORY. 2 vols., 21s.

FRIEDEMANN BACH; or, The Fortunes of an Idealist. Adapted from the German of A. E. BRACHVOGEL. By the Rev. J. WALKER, B.C.L. Dedicated, with permission, to H.R.H. the PRINCESS CHRISTIAN of SCHLESWIG-HOLSTEIN. 1 vol., crown 8vo, 7s. 6d.

GAUNT ABBEY. By ELIZABETH J. LYSAGHT, Author of "Building upon Sand," "Nearer and Dearer," etc. 3 vols., 31s. 6d.

GOLD DUST. A Story. 3 vols., 31s. 6d.

GOLDEN MEMORIES. By EFFIE LEIGH. 2 vols., 21s.

GRAYWORTH: a Story of Country Life. By CAREY HAZELWOOD. 3 vols., 31s. 6d.

Samuel Tinsley, 10, Southampton Street, Strand.

GRANTHAM SECRETS. By Phœbe M. Feilden 3 vols. 31s. 6d.

GREED'S LABOUR LOST. By the Author of "Recommended to Mercy," etc. 3 vols., 31s. 6d.

HER GOOD NAME. By J. Fortrey Bouverie. 3 vols., 31s. 6d.

HER IDOL. By Maxwell Hood. 3 vols., 31s. 6d.

HILDA AND I. By Mrs. Winchcombe Hartley. 2 vols., 21s.

"An interesting, well-written, and natural story."—*Public Opinion.*

HILLESDEN ON THE MOORS. By Rosa Mackenzie Kettle, Author of "The Mistress of Langdale Hall." 2 vols., 21s.

HIS LITTLE COUSIN. By Emma Maria Pearson, Author of "One Love in a Life." 3 vols., 31s. 6d.

IN BONDS, BUT FETTERLESS: a Tale of Old Ulster. By Richard Cuninghame. 2 vols., 21s.

IN SECRET PLACES. By Robert J. Griffiths, LL.D. 3 vols., 31s. 6d.

IN SPITE OF FORTUNE. By Maurice Gay. 3 vols., 31s. 6d.

IS IT FOR EVER? By Kate Mainwaring. 3 vols., 31s. 6d.

JOHN FENN'S WIFE. By Maria Lewis. Crown 8vo., 7s. 6d.

KATE BYRNE. By S. Howard Taylor. 2 vols., 21s.

KATE RANDAL'S BARGAIN. By Mrs. Eiloart, Author of "The Curate's Discipline," "Some of Our Girls," "Meg," &c. 3 vols., 31s. 6d.

Samuel Tinsley, 10, Southampton Street, Strand.

Samuel Tinsley's Publications. 7

KITTY'S RIVAL. By SYDNEY MOSTYN, Author of 'The Surgeon's Secret,' etc. 3 vols., 31s. 6d.

"Essentially dramatic and absorbing. . . . . We have nothing but unqualified praise for 'Kitty's Rival.'"—*Public Opinion*.

LADY LOUISE. By KATHLEEN ISABELLE CLARGES. 3 vols., 31s. 6d.

LALAGE. By AUGUSTA CHAMBERS. Crown 8vo, 7s. 6d.

LASCARE: a Tale. 3 vols., 31s. 6d.

LEAVES FROM AN OLD PORTFOLIO. By ELIZA MARY BARRON. Crown 8vo, 7s. 6d.

LORD CASTLETON'S WARD. By Mrs. B. R. GREEN. 3 vols., 31s. 6d.

"Mrs. Green has written a novel which will hold the reader entranced from the first page to the last."—*Morning Post*.

MARGARET MORTIMER'S SECOND HUSBAND. By Mrs. HILLS. 1 vol., 7s. 6d.

MARRIED FOR MONEY. 1 vol., 10s. 6d.

"Well written, and full of incident. . . . . . those persons, therefore, who like to be carried on quickly from one event to another, will certainly get what they want in 'Married for Money.'"— *Western Morning News*.

"Characters are sketched with some degree of power, and there is no little ingenuity in the way in which the final catastrophe is contrived.—*Scotsman*.

"Far from ill-written, or uninteresting."—*Graphic*.

MART AND MANSION: a Tale of Struggle and Rest. By PHILIP MASSINGER. 3 vols., 31s. 6d.

MARY GRAINGER: A Story. By GEORGE LEIGH. 2 vols., 21s.

MR. VAUGHAN'S HEIR. By FRANK LEE BENEDICT, Author of "Miss Dorothy's Charge," etc. 3 vols., 31s. 6d.

MUSICAL TALES, PHANTASMS, AND SKETCHES. From the German of ELISE POLKO. Dedicated (with permission) to Sir Julius Benedict. Crown 8vo, 7s. 6d.

NEARER AND DEARER. By ELIZABETH J. LYSAGHT, Author of "Building upon Sand." 3 vols., 31s. 6d.

Samuel Tinsley, 10, Southampton Street. Strand.

NEGLECTED; a Story of Nursery Education Forty Years Ago. By Miss JULIA LUARD. Crown 8vo., 5s. cloth.

NO FATHERLAND. By MADAME VON OPPEN. 2 vols., 21s.

NORTONDALE CASTLE. 1 vol., 7s. 6d.

NOT TO BE BROKEN. By W. A. CHANDLER. Crown 8vo., 10s. 6d.

ONE FOR ANOTHER. By EMMA C. WAIT. Crown 8vo, 7s. 6d.

ONLY SEA AND SKY. By ELIZABETH HINDLEY. 2 vols., 21s.

OVER THE FURZE. By ROSA M. KETTLE, Author of the "Mistress of Langdale Hall," etc. 3 vols., 31s. 6d.

PERCY LOCKHART. By F. W. BAXTER. 2 vols., 21s.

PUTTYPUT'S PROTÉGÉE; or, Road, Rail, and River. A Story in Three Books. By HENRY GEORGE CHURCHILL. Crown 8vo., (uniform with "The Mistress of Langdale Hall"), with 14 illustrations by WALLIS MACKAY. Post free, 4s. Second edition.

"It is a lengthened and diversified farce, full of screaming fun and comic delineation—a reflection of Dickens, Mrs. Malaprop, and Mr. Boucicault, and dealing with various descriptions of social life. We have read and laughed, pooh-poohed, and read again, ashamed of our interest, but our interest has been too strong for our shame. Readers may do worse than surrender themselves to its melo-dramatic enjoyment. From title-page to colophon, only Dominie Sampson's epithet can describe it- it is 'prodigious.'"—*British Quarterly Review.*

RAVENSDALE. By ROBERT THYNNE, Author of "Tom Delany." 3 vols., 31s. 6d.

"A well-told, natural, and wholesome story."—*Standard.*
"No one can deny merit to the writer."—*Saturday Review.*

RUPERT REDMOND: A Tale of England, Ireland, and America. By WALTER SIMS SOUTHWELL. 3 vols., 31s. 6d.

Samuel Tinsley, 10, Southampton Street, Strand.

Samuel Tinsley's Publications.

SAINT SIMON'S NIECE. By Frank Lee Benedict, Author of "Miss Dorothy's Charge." 3 vols., 31s. 6d.

From the **Spectator**, July 24th:—"A new and powerful novelist has arisen ... We rejoice to recognise a new novelist of real genius, who knows and depicts powerfully some of the most striking and overmastering passions of the human heart ... It is seldom that we rise from the perusal of a story with the sense of excitement which Mr. Benedict has produced."

From the **Scotsman**, June 11th:—"Mr. Frank Lee Benedict may not be generally recognised as such, but he is one of the cleverest living novelists of the school of which Miss Braddon was the founder and remains the chief. He is fond of a 'strong' plot, and besprinkles his stories abundantly with startling incidents ... The story is written with remarkable ability, and its interest is thoroughly well sustained."

SELF-UNITED. By Mrs. Hickes Bryant. 3 vols., 31s. 6d.

Westminster Review:—"'Self-United' has many marks of no ordinary kind ... The style is excellent, the conversation bright and natural, the plot good, and the interest well sustained up to the last moment."

SHINGLEBOROUGH SOCIETY. 3 vols., 31s. 6d.

SIR MARMADUKE LORTON. By the Hon. A. S. G. Canning. 3 vols., 31s. 6d.

SKYWARD AND EARTHWARD: a Tale. By Arthur Penrice. 1 vol., crown 8vo, 7s. 6d.

SPOILT LIVES. By Mrs. Raper. Crown 8vo, 7s. 6d.

SOME OF OUR GIRLS. By Mrs. Eiloart, Author of "The Curate's Discipline," "The Love that Lived," "Meg," etc., etc. 3 vols., 31s. 6d.

"A book that should be read."—*Athenæum*.

SONS OF DIVES. 2 vols., 21s.

SQUIRE HARRINGTON'S SECRET. By George W. Garrett. 2 vols., 21s.

STANLEY MEREDITH: a Tale. By "Sabina." Crown 8vo, 7s. 6d.

STRANDED, BUT NOT LOST. By Dorothy Bromyard. 3 vols., 31s. 6d.

SWEET IDOLATRY. By Miss Anstruther. Crown 8vo, 7s. 6d.

Samuel Tinsley, 10, Southampton Street, Strand.

THE ADVENTURES OF MICK CALLIGHIN, M.P., a Story of Home Rule; and THE DE BURGHOS, a Romance. By W. R. ANCKETILL. In one Volume, with Illustrations. Crown 8vo, 7s. 6d.

THE BARONET'S CROSS. By MARY MEEKE, Author of "Marion's Path through Shadow to Sunshine." 2 vols., 21s.

THE BRITISH SUBALTERN. By an Ex-SUBALTERN. 1 vol., 7s. 6d.

THE D'EYNCOURTS OF FAIRLEIGH. By THOMAS ROWLAND SKEMP. 3 vols., 31s. 6d.

THE HEIR OF REDDESMONT. 3 vols., 31s. 6d.

THE INSIDIOUS THIEF: a Tale for Humble Folks. By One of Themselves. Crown 8vo, 5s. Second Edition.

THE LOVE THAT LIVED. By Mrs. EILOART, Author of "The Curate's Discipline," "Just a Woman," "Woman's Wrong," &c. 3 vols., 31s. 6d.

"Three volumes which most people will prefer not to leave till they have read the last page of the third volume."—*Pall Mall Gazette.*

"One of the most thoroughly wholesome novels we have read for some time."—*Scotsman.*

THE MAGIC OF LOVE. By Mrs. FORREST-GRANT, Author of "Fair, but not Wise." 3 vols., 31s. 6d.

"A very amusing novel."—*Scotsman.*

THE MISTRESS OF LANGDALE HALL: a Romance of the West Riding. By ROSA MACKENZIE KETTLE. Complete in one handsome volume, with Frontispiece and Vignette by PERCIVAL SKELTON. 4s., post free.

"The story is interesting and very pleasantly written, and for the sake of both author and publisher we cordially wish it the reception it deserves." —*Saturday Review.*

THE SECRET OF TWO HOUSES. By FANNY FISHER. 2 vols., 21s.

THE SEDGEBOROUGH WORLD. By A. FAREBROTHER. 2 vols., 21s.

THE SHADOW OF ERKSDALE. By BOURTON MARSHALL. 3 vols, 31s. 6d.

Samuel Tinsley, 10, Southampton Street, Strand.

Samuel Tinsley's Publications. 11

THE SURGEON'S SECRET. By SYDNEY MOSTYN, Author of "Kitty's Rival," etc. Crown 8vo., 10s. 6d.

"A most exciting novel—the best on our list. It may be fairly recommended as a very extraordinary book."—*John Bull.*

THE THORNTONS OF THORNBURY. By Mrs. HENRY LOWTHER CHERMSIDE. 3 vols., 31s. 6d.

THE TRUE STORY OF HUGH NOBLE'S FLIGHT. By the Authoress of "What Her Face Said." 10s. 6d.

"A pleasant story, with touches of exquisite pathos, well told by one who is master of an excellent and sprightly style."—*Standard.*

THE WIDOW UNMASKED; or, the Firebrand in the Family. By FLORA F. WYLDE. 3 vols., 31s. 6d.

TIMOTHY CRIPPLE; or, "Life's a Feast." By THOMAS AURIOL ROBINSON. 2 vols., 21s.

"This is a most amusing book, and the author deserves great credit for the novelty of his design, and the quaint humour with which it is worked out."—*Public Opinion.*

TIM'S CHARGE. By AMY CAMPBELL. 1 vol., crown 8vo, 7s. 6d.

TOO LIGHTLY BROKEN. 3 vols., 31s. 6d.

"A very pleasing story . . . . . very prettily told."—*Morning Post.*

TOM DELANY. By ROBERT THYNNE, Author of "Ravensdale." 3 vols., 31s. 6d.

"A very bright, healthy, simply-told story."—*Standard.*

"All the individuals whom the reader meets at the gold-fields are well-drawn, amongst whom not the least interesting is 'Terrible Mac.'"—*Hour*

"There is not a dull page in the book."—*Scotsman.*

TOWER HALLOWDEANE. 2 vols., 21s.

TOXIE: a Tale. 3 vols., 31s. 6d.

TWIXT CUP and LIP. By MARY LOVETT-CAMERON. 3 vols., 31s. 6d.

"Displays signs of more than ordinary promise. . . . As a whole the novel cannot fail to please. Its plot is one that will arrest attention; and its characters, one and all, are full of life and have that nameless charm which at once attracts and retains the sympathy of the reader."—*Daily News.*

Samuel Tinsley, 10, Southampton Street, Strand.

Samuel Tinsley's Publications.

'TWIXT WIFE AND FATHERLAND. 2 vols., 21s.

"A bright, vigorous, and healthy story, and decidedly above the average of books of this class. Being in two volumes it commands the reader's unbroken attention to the very end."—*Standard.*

"It is by someone who has caught her (Baroness Tautphoeus') gift of telling a charming story in the boldest manner, and of forcing us to take an interest in her characters, which writers, far better from a literary point of view, can never approach."—*Athenæum.*

TWO STRIDES OF DESTINY. By S. BROOKES BUCKLEE. 3 vols., 31s. 6d.

UNDER PRESSURE. By T. E. PEMBERTON. 2 vols., 21s.

WAGES: a Story in Three Books. 3 vols., 31s. 6d.

WANDERING FIRES. By Mrs. M. C. DESPARD, Author of "Chaste as Ice," &c. 3 vols., 31s. 6d.

WEBS OF LOVE. (I. A Lawyer's Device. II. Sancta Simplicitas.) By G. E. H. 1 vol., Crown 8vo., 10s. 6d.

WEIMAR'S TRUST. By Mrs. EDWARD CHRISTIAN. 3 vols., 31s. 6d.

WHO CAN TELL? By A MERE HAZARD. Crown 8vo, 7s. 6d.

WILL SHE BEAR IT? A Tale of the Weald. 3 vols., 31s. 6d.

* "This is a clever story, easily and naturally told, and the reader's interest sustained throughout. . . . A pleasant, readable book, such as we can heartily recommend."—*Spectator.*

WOMAN'S AMBITION. By M. L. LYONS. 1 vol., 7s. 6d.

THIRTIETH THOUSAND.

YE VAMPYRES! A Legend of the National Betting Ring, showing what became of it. By the SPECTRE. In striking Illustrated Cover, price 2s., post free.

Samuel Tinsley, 10, Southampton Street, Strand.

ROBA D'ITALIA; or, Italian Lights and Shadows: a record of Travel. By CHARLES W. HECKETHORN. In 2 vols., 8vo, price 30s.

THE EMPEROR AND THE GALILEAN: an Historical Drama. Translated from the Norwegian of HENRIK IBSEN, by CATHERINE RAY. In 1 vol., crown 8vo, 7s. 6d.

ETYMONIA. In 1 vol., crown 8vo, 7s. 6d.

HOW I SPENT MY TWO YEARS' LEAVE; or, My Impressions of the Mother Country, the Continent of Europe, the United States of America, and Canada. By an Indian Officer. In one vol. 8vo. Handsomely bound. Price 12s.

FACT AGAINST FICTION. The Habits and Treatment of Animals Practically Considered. Hydrophobia and Distemper. With some remarks on Darwin. By the HON. GRANTLEY F. BERKELEY. 2 vols., 8vo., 30s.

MALTA SIXTY YEARS AGO. With a Concise History of the Order of St. John of Jerusalem, the Crusades, and Knights Templars. By Col. CLAUDIUS SHAW. Handsomely bound in cloth, 10s. 6d., gilt edges, 12s.

ON THE MISMANAGEMENT OF THE PUBLIC RECORD OFFICE. By J. PYM YEATMAN, Barrister-at-Law. In Wrapper, price 1s.

LETTER TO THE QUEEN ON HER RETIREMENT FROM PUBLIC LIFE. By One of Her Majesty's most Loyal Subjects. In wrapper, price 1s., post free.

THE USE AND ABUSE OF IRRATIONAL ANIMALS; with some Remarks on the Essential Moral Difference between Genuine "Sport" and the Horrors of Vivisection. In wrapper, price 1s.

CONFESSIONS OF A WEST-END USURER. In Illustrated Cover, price 1s.

THE TICHBORNE AND ORTON AUTOGRAPHS; comprising Autograph Letters of Roger Tichborne, Arthur Orton (to Mary Ann Loder), and the Defendant (early letters to Lady Tichborne, &c.), in facsimile. In wrapper, price 6d.

Samuel Tinsley, 10, Southampton Street, Strand.

HARRY'S BIG BOOTS: a Fairy Tale, for "Smalle Folke." By S. E. GAY. With 8 Full-page Illustrations and a Vignette by the author, drawn on wood by PERCIVAL SKELTON. Crown 8vo., handsomely bound in cloth, price 5s.

"Some capital fun will be found in 'Harry's Big Boots.'... The illustrations are excellent, and so is the story."—*Pall Mall Gazette.*

MOVING EARS. By the Ven. Archdeacon WEAKHEAD, Rector of Newtown, Kent. 1 vol., crown 8vo., 5s.

A TRUE FLEMISH STORY. By the Author of "The Eve of St. Nicholas." In wrapper, 1s.

THE PHYSIOLOGY OF THE SECTS. Crown 8vo., price 5s.

ANOTHER WORLD; or, Fragments from the Star City of Montalluyah. By HERMES. Third Edition, revised, with additions. Post 8vo., price 12s.

THE FALL OF MAN: An Answer to Mr. Darwin's "Descent of Man;" being a Complete Refutation, by common-sense arguments, of the Theory of Natural Selection. 1s., sewed.

THE RITUALIST'S PROGRESS; or, A Sketch of the Reforms and Ministrations of the Rev. Septimus Alban, Member of the E.C.U., Vicar of S. Alicia, Sloperton. By A B WILDERED Parishioner. Fcp. 8vo. 2s. 6d. cloth.

MISTRESSES AND MAIDS. By HUBERT CURTIS, Author of "Helen," etc. Price 1d.

EPITAPHIANA; or, the Curiosities of Churchyard Literature: being a Miscellaneous Collection of Epitaphs, with an INTRODUCTION. By W. FAIRLEY. Crown 8vo., cloth, price 5s. Post free.

"Entertaining."—*Pall Mall Gazette.*
"A capital collection."—*Court Circular.*
"A very readable volume."—*Daily Review.*
"A most interesting book."—*Leeds Mercury.*
"Interesting and amusing." *Nonconformist.*
"Particularly entertaining."—*Public Opinion.*
"A curious and entertaining volume."—*Oxford Chronicle.*
'A very interesting collection."—*Civil Service Gazette.*

TWELVE NATIONAL BALLADS (First Series). Dedicated to Liberals of all classes. By PHILHELOT, of Cambridge; in ornamental cover, price sixpence, post free.

Samuel Tinsley, 10, Southampton Street, Strand.

POEMS AND SONNETS. By H. GREENHOUGH SMITH, B.A. Fcap, 8vo, 3s. 6d.

GRANADA, AND OTHER POEMS. By M. SABISTON. Fcp. 8vo., 4s.

THE DEATH OF ÆGEUS, and other Poems. By W. H. A. EMRA. Fcp. 8vo., 5s.

HELEN, and other Poems. By HUBERT CURTIS. Fcp. 8vo., 3s. 6d.

MISPLACED LOVE. A Tale of Love, Sin, Sorrow, and Remorse. 1 vol., crown 8vo., 5s.

THE SOUL SPEAKS, and other Poems. By FRANCIS H. HEMERY. In wrapper, 1s.

SUMMER SHADE AND WINTER SUNSHINE: Poems. By ROSA MACKENZIE KETTLE, Author of "The Mistress of Langdale Hall." New Edition. 2s. 6d., cloth.

THE WITCH of NEMI, and other Poems. By EDWARD BRENNAN. Crown 8vo., 10s. 6d.

MARY DESMOND, AND OTHER POEMS. By NICHOLAS J. GANNON. Fcp. 8vo., 4s., cloth. Second Edition.

THE GOLDEN PATH: a Poem. By ISABELLA STUART. 6d., sewed.

THE REDBREAST OF CANTERBURY CATHEDRAL: Lines from the Latin of Peter du Moulin, sometime a Prebendary of Canterbury. Translated by the Rev. F. B. WELLS, M.A., Rector of Woodchurch. Handsomely bound, price 1s.

BALAK AND BALAAM IN EUROPEAN COSTUME. By the Rev. JAMES KEAN, M.A., Assistant to the Incumbent of Markinch, Fife. 6d., sewed.

ANOTHER ROW AT DAME EUROPA'S SCHOOL. Showing how John's Cook made an IRISH STEW, and what came of it. 6d., sewed.

Samuel Tinsley, 10, Southampton Street, Strand.

Samuel Tinsley's Publications.

NOTICE.—SECOND EDITION.

UNTRODDEN SPAIN, and her Black Country. Being Sketches of the Life and Character of the Spaniard of the Interior. By HUGH JAMES ROSE, M.A., of Oriel College, Oxford; Chaplain to the English, French, and German Mining Companies of Linaries; and formerly Acting Chaplain to Her Majesty's Forces at Dover Garrison. In 2 vols., 8vo., price 30s.

The Times says—"These volumes form a very pleasing commentary on a land and a people to which Englishmen will always turn with sympathetic interest."

The Saturday Review says—"His title of 'Untrodden Spain' is no misnomer. He leads us into scenes and among classes of Spaniards where few English writers have preceded him. . . . We can only recommend our readers to get it and search for themselves. Those who are most intimately acquainted with Spain will best appreciate its varied excellences."

The Spectator says—"The author's kindliness is as conspicuous as his closeness of observation and fairness of judgment; his sympathy with the people inspires his pen as happily as does his artistic appreciation of the country; and both have combined in the production of a work of striking novelty and sterling value."

The Athenæum says—"We regret that we cannot make further extracts, for 'Untrodden Spain' is by far the best book upon Spanish peasant life that we have ever met with."

The Literary Churchman says—"Seldom has a book of travel come before us which has so taken our fancy in reading, and left behind it, when the reading was over, so distinct an impression."

OVER THE BORDERS OF CHRISTENDOM AND ESLAMIAH; or, Travels in the Summer of 1875 through Hungary, Slavonia, Bosnia, Servia, Herzegovina, Dalmatia, and Montenegro to the North of Albania. By JAMES CREAGH, Author of "A Scamper to Sebastopol." 2 vols., large post 8vo, 25s.

ITALY REVISITED. By A. GALLENGA (of *The Times*), Author of "Country Life in Piedmont," &c., &c. 2 vols., 8vo., price 30s.

CANTON AND THE BOGUE: the Narrative of an Eventful Six Months in China. By WALTER WILLIAM MUNDY. Crown 8vo, 7s. 6d.

DICKENS'S LONDON: or, London in the Works of Charles Dickens. By T. EDGAR PEMBERTON, Author of "Under Pressure." Crown 8vo, 6s.

Samuel Tinsley, 10, Southampton Street, Strand.

www.ingramcontent.com/pod-product-compliance
Lightning Source LLC
Chambersburg PA
CBHW020841160426
43192CB00007B/742